COAL AND CANADA-U.S. ENERGY RELATIONS

Richard L. Gordon

Canadian–American Committee

SPONSORED BY

C. D. HOWE RESEARCH INSTITUTE (CANADA
NATIONAL PLANNING ASSOCIATION (U.S.A

THE CANADIAN-AMERICAN COMMITTEE

The Canadian-American Committee was established in 1957 to study and discuss the broad range of economic factors affecting the relationship between Canada and the United States. Its members are business, labour, agricultural, and professional leaders from the private sector who have direct involvement and experience in relations between the two countries. There is approximately equal membership from both nations, with the objective of obtaining representative views from the major geographic regions and industrial sectors in each. The Committee is sponsored by two non-profit research organizations — the National Planning Association in the United States and the C. D. Howe Research Institute in Canada, described on the inside back cover.

The Committee believes that the maintenance of a cooperative relationship between Canada and the United States is essential to, and in the best interests of, both countries. At the same time, the Committee recognizes that this relationship is evolving and that this evolution may produce occasional strains and conflicts. The Committee seeks to encourage greater public understanding of the nature of the relationship and the issues that have arisen, or may arise, with this relationship and attempts to develop and disseminate ideas for constructive policy responses to these issues that are consistent with the national goals of the two countries.

In pursuit of the objective of encouraging greater public understanding, the Committee sponsors objective research studies on various aspects of Canadian-American relations. These studies are prepared by experts in both countries and, with the Committee's approval, are published. On the basis of these factual studies and of discussions at its meeting, the Committee also issues policy statements signed by its members. A partial listing of the Committee publications is given on page 75.

The Canadian-American Committee is a unique organization in terms of both its broadly diversified membership from the private sector and its sponsorship of a coordinated publication program combining factual studies and policy-oriented statements on Canadian-American relations. It meets twice a year, once in Canada and once in the United States, and these meetings provide an opportunity for members to discuss a wide range of topics with senior government officials, scholars, and other people with a specialized knowledge of the relationship. The work of the Committee is financed by funds contributed from private sources in the two countries. Foundation grants made it possible to initiate the Committee and are an additional source of financing for specific research studies undertaken by the Committee.

Offices on behalf of the Committee are maintained at 1606 New Hampshire Avenue, N.W., Washington, D.C. 20009, and at 2064 Sun Life Building, Montreal, Quebec H3B 2X7. Norman Mogil, in Montreal, and John Volpe, in Washington, are the Directors of Research.

Robert M. MacIntosh   Richard J. Schmeelk

Co-Chairmen of the Committee

COAL AND CANADA-U.S. ENERGY RELATIONS

Richard L. Gordon

CANADIAN-AMERICAN COMMITTEE
sponsored by
C. D. Howe Research Institute (Canada)
National Planning Association (U.S.A.)

76- 7446
Legal Deposit — 2nd Quarter 1976
Quebec National Library
Library of Congress Catalogue Number 76-20420
ISBN 0-88806-017-3
June, 1976, $3.00
Quotation with appropriate credit is permissible
C. D. Howe Research Institute (Montreal, Quebec) and
National Planning Association (Washington, D.C.)
Printed in Canada

STATEMENT
BY THE CANADIAN-AMERICAN COMMITTEE
ON *Coal and Canada-U.S. Energy Relations*
by Richard L. Gordon

As North America seeks ways to meet its energy needs for the future, coal has emerged as a potential alternative to growing dependence on imported oil. Coal represents the largest and most readily accessible source of energy available in the continental United States. Although operating from a much smaller reserve base, Canada, too, is looking forward to the time when its coal deposits will begin to make a greater contribution to its domestic energy requirements. Coal can be consumed directly or converted into synthetic oil and gas, although currently available technologies for making this conversion do not appear to be commercially attractive.

Both Canada and the United States export substantial volumes of coal to countries throughout the world. Canadian exports of coking coal, an essential ingredient in steel-making, are concentrated in the west and principally go to Japan. The comparative costs have made it economically attractive for Canada to rely heavily upon coal imports from the United States to fuel electrical utilities in Ontario and to provide coking coal for domestic steel mills. Some Canadians have expressed concern that this reliance on U.S. coal supplies has made Canada vulnerable to disruptive cutbacks in supplies should the United States decide that its coal must be reserved to meet domestic energy needs.

Recognizing the importance of coal in the overall North American energy picture and its special significance in Canada-U.S. energy trade, the Canadian-American Committee commissioned a study to explore the prospects for coal production and trade. In commissioning this study, the Committee had two general purposes in mind. First, it felt that there was a need for a basic coal survey that would marshall the available facts and provide an appraisal of the opportunities for developing these seemingly large coal reserves in each country. Second, the Committee sought to obtain an expert evaluation of Canadian fears about the availability of U.S. coal supplies in the future.

The author chosen for this assignment was Professor Richard L. Gordon, a mineral economist with The Pennsylvania State University's College of Earth and Mineral Science. Professor Gordon has been involved actively in coal research and analysis for several years and is the author of a number of published studies in the area.

Professor Gordon has examined, in this study, a number of critical factors that bear directly on the longer-run demand and supply balance for coal, including:

- the quantity and quality of coal reserves in each country;
- public policies, including those governing land use, environmental standards, taxation, and private ownership in the coal industry; and
- the probable longer-term cost of supplying coal and the comparative costs of other fossil fuels as well as nuclear energy.

In preparing this survey of the facts and issues bearing on the development of new coal reserves in each country, Professor Gordon arrived at two major conclusions regarding the role of coal in future Canada-U.S. energy relations.

- First, the prospects of a major revival in the use of coal as an alternative energy source remain in considerable doubt, especially in the United States. To begin with, too little is known about the nature and extent of reserves and their adequacy in light of future energy needs. Moreover, the outlook for U.S. coal depends critically on how a number of policy issues are resolved, particularly in the area of environmental control. Finally, as a primary source of fuel in the generation of electricity, coal will face considerable competitive cost pressures from other fossil fuels and from nuclear energy.

- Second, although the United States will be increasing its coal consumption well into the 1980s, this development is not expected to lead necessarily to a curtailment of exports to Canada. Moreover, the presence of a number of benefits to the United States arising from these exports makes it unlikely that the United States would resort to restricting them.

This study is one of a continuing series, the purpose of which is to gather together the available facts on specific energy subjects of interest to both countries and to present these facts in an interesting and informative fashion to the general reader. In the future, the Committee intends to examine aspects of the Canada-U.S. interchange of electrical power and the outlook for uranium and nuclear power in each country.

In the Committee's view, this study attests to the fact that there are no simple and easy solutions to the development of new energy sources. A much greater reliance on coal as a major energy source of the future cannot be substantiated by the facts currently available. For this reason, the Committee recommends that both countries give greater priority to tackling their medium- and longer-range energy problems.

Professor Gordon's analysis and conclusions regarding coal developments are his own. As is customary, the Canadian-American Committee does not necessarily endorse them but does recommend the publication of this study in the belief that it offers an intelligent contribution to greater public understanding of an important aspect of energy concerns in both countries.

MEMBERS OF THE CANADIAN-AMERICAN COMMITTEE SIGNING THE STATEMENT

Co-Chairmen

ROBERT M. MacINTOSH
Executive Vice-President, The Bank of Nova Scotia

RICHARD J. SCHMEELK
Partner, Salomon Brothers

Members

JOHN N. ABELL
Vice President and Director, Wood Gundy Limited

*R. L. ADAMS
Executive Vice President, Continental Oil Company

J. A. ARMSTRONG
President and Chief Executive Officer, Imperial Oil Limited

IAN A. BARCLAY
Chairman and Chief Executive Officer, British Columbia Forest Products Limited

MICHEL BELANGER
President, Provincial Bank of Canada

ROY F. BENNETT
President and Chief Executive Officer, Ford Motor Company of Canada, Limited

ROD J. BILODEAU
Chairman of the Board, Honeywell Limited

*ROBERT BLAIR
President and Chief Executive Officer, Alberta Gas Trunk Line Company Limited

J. E. BRENT
Chairman of the Board, IBM Canada Ltd.

PHILIP BRIGGS
Senior Vice President, Metropolitan Life Insurance Company

ARDEN BURBIDGE
Burbidge Farm, Park River, North Dakota

NICHOLAS J. CAMPBELL, JR.
Director and Senior Vice President, Exxon Corporation

SHIRLEY CARR
Executive Vice-President, Canadian Labour Congress

W. R. CLERIHUE
Executive Vice-President, Staff and Administration, Celanese Corporation

HON. JOHN V. CLYNE
MacMillan Bloedel Limited

*THOMAS E. COVEL
Marion, Massachusetts

J. S. DEWAR
President, Union Carbide Canada Limited

JOHN H. DICKEY
President, Nova Scotia Pulp Limited

THOMAS W. diZEREGA
Vice President, Northwest Pipeline Corporation

WILLIAM DODGE
Ottawa, Ontario

A. D. DUNTON
Professor and Director, Institute of Canadian Studies, Carleton University

STEPHEN C. EYRE
Comptroller, First National City Bank, New York, New York

A. J. FISHER
President, Fiberglas Canada Limited

ROBERT M. FOWLER
President, C. D. Howe Research Institute

JOHN F. GALLAGHER
Vice President, International Operations, Sears, Roebuck and Company

CARL J. GILBERT
Dover, Massachusetts

PAT GREATHOUSE
Vice President, International Union, UAW

A. D. HAMILTON
President and Chief Executive Officer, Domtar Limited

R. A. IRWIN
Chairman, Consolidated-Bathurst Limited

EDGAR F. KAISER, JR.
President and Chief Executive Officer, Kaiser Resources Ltd.

DONALD P. KELLY
President and Chief Operating Officer, Esmark, Inc.

DAVID KIRK
Executive Secretary, The Canadian Federation of Agriculture

J. L. KUHN
President and General Manager, 3M Canada Limited

HERBERT H. LANK
Director, Du Pont of Canada Limited

PAUL LEMAN
President, Alcan Aluminium Limited

FRANKLIN A. LINDSAY
Chairman, Itek Corporation

L. H. LORRAIN
President, Canadian Paperworkers Union

M. W. MACKENZIE
Vice Chairman, Canron Limited

WILLIAM MAHONEY
National Director, United Steelworkers of America, AFL-CIO-CLC

v

*See Footnotes to the Statement, page 71.

CONTENTS

Tables

1

Introduction

There is widespread concern in North America about the adequacy of future supplies of energy to maintain economic growth without undue dependence on oil imports. Many have assumed that coal resources, particularly in the United States, could be developed rapidly to compensate for dwindling domestic oil and gas reserves and thus to reduce the need to rely on imported oil. This study will attempt to examine the validity of this assumption, although there are serious inadequacies in the data on which this assessment must be based.

In contrast to its role as a major oil importer, the United States has long been the world's predominant coal-exporting country. All nations that rely upon the United States for coal are concerned about the possible impact of increased U.S. consumption of its coal resources on the continued availability of these exports.

This potential problem appears particularly acute for Canada because the United States is the sole source of Canadian coal imports, providing over half of Canadian requirements. Steel mills in Ontario are almost totally dependent on U.S. metallurgical coal, and Ontario Hydro is heavily reliant on U.S. steam coal. Canada, concerned about the availability of both types of coal over the longer run, has had to consider the possible role of coal resources in western Canada in overcoming any potential future reduction in the flow of U.S. coal to Ontario users. This study will also examine coal in the context of Canadian-American energy relationships and try to appraise the validity of Canadian concerns about future U.S. coal exports.

Focus of Study

The approach used in this study is twofold:

- First, I consider the actual prospects of coal as a major alternative to oil, natural gas, and possibly nuclear power in the coming decades. Appraisals are made of how much coal is likely to be used and the specific forms this use will take. The options for coal include

1

use in traditional forms, changes into relatively simple synthetic fuels, and transformation into synthetic crude oil or methane (the chemical name for what is popularly called natural gas).[1] In its traditional role, coal might continue to be burned to raise steam in large industrial boilers, primarily in electric-power plants, and to manufacture coke used in pig iron production. Environmental problems might be solved by removing pollutants after combustion or by shifting to coal that produces tolerably low levels of air pollution. A radically different concept would be to use coal to produce large amounts of synthetic crude oil and methane. An intermediate view is that it would be desirable to develop synthetics that are simpler than crude oil and methane. Such synthetics might provide a cheaper way to meet the controls on air pollution by industrial boilers, with the pollutants' being removed more easily during the synthesis process than by post-combustion cleaning. At any rate, the options are varied, and the combinations offer interesting, albeit complex, considerations for energy policy-makers over the next two decades or more.

• Second, having made such an appraisal for the U.S. coal industry, I then turn to its implications for Canadian customers. A key concern is whether traditional sources of coal from the United States will become "unavailable" as a result of changes in U.S. coal demand and supply conditions. "Unavailability" is an imprecise concept and often quite inappropriate for explaining economic problems. In the uncontrolled marketplace, when demand puts pressure on supplies, prices rise, and those with the least pressing demands (i.e., those unwilling or unable to pay the new higher price) find their supplies bid away by those willing to pay higher prices. Of course, those priced out of the market may exert political pressures on the government to intervene to restore their supplies.

These arguments imply that the basic Canadian concern over availability of U.S. coal has two elements — a fear of being priced out of the market and some trepidation that, even if Canadian consumers are willing to pay higher prices, political pressures will arise to prohibit the exports. The issue is complicated because Canada has substantial needs for both "metallurgical" and "steam" coal from the United States (meaning, respectively, coal with special properties suitable for use in the manufacture of the coke essential for pig iron production and coal burned directly as a source of heat). To the extent that the supply-demand relationships may develop differently for the two types of coal, Canada may experience quite a different set of problems in securing supplies of each. In any event, should supply restrictions become apparent, Canada obviously must consider its options wisely and well in advance of any eventualities.

---

[1] The technical term "synthetic methane" is used here in preference to the popular but logically absurd terminology "synthetic natural gas."

One such option examined in this study concerns the replacement of some U.S.-supplied coal through a massive development program to exploit Canada's own significant coal reserves in western Canada. But, as my analysis suggests, this should not be considered to be the only — or, for that matter, the most economically feasible — alternative available to Canada if the present flow of U.S. coal becomes impaired. U.S. supplies could possibly be replaced with coal from non-traditional reserves, such as those found in the Great Plain states of Wyoming, Montana, North Dakota, and Utah. Moreover, it is not at all certain that, in future, coal costs in Canada and the United States will be competitive with those of substitute fuels, such as nuclear energy.

One reason that the future is so uncertain concerns the potentially great, but unpredictable, role that technology will play in shaping the course of supply and demand in coming decades. For example, it is possible that, should the supply of U.S. metallurgical coal be curtailed, the use of Canadian metallurgical coal reserves would not be the preferred solution. Research is progressing on developing alternative coking techniques that allow for much greater flexibility in the choice of coal; in fact, some processes already exist for producing pig iron without the use of coke.

Limiting Factors

Coal is but one of many available or potential energy sources; therefore, some effort must be made to compare the relative positions of these alternative sources. However, our ability to forecast the price and future availability of these alternative energy supplies is constrained by a number of important considerations.

The basic problem in energy forecasting is that our knowledge of the remaining endowments of worldwide energy resources is quite poor. Information about such matters as the quality of available resources and the ease with which such resources can be extracted is seriously inadequate. This situation is a natural consequence of many years of ample energy supplies, during which low-cost energy sources managed to appear whenever they were needed and the world thought it could afford to get along with scanty resource data. Nature gives scanty clues about the existence of minerals. Extensive activity to explore for, and develop, resources is necessary to "prove" reserves — i.e., to learn how much of the mineral exists, what technologies are required for efficient extraction, and what the cost will be. For fuels other than coal, only that portion of the discovery that appears economically recoverable is reported as proved reserves. The process of proving reserves is expensive, and as long as energy was cheap and abundant, the proving of more reserves than were needed to support current production did not seem to be necessary or justified.

One of the great ironies of current energy discussions has been the rash of demagogic attacks on the petroleum industry for "concealing" reserves data. In fact, the industry has done an exemplary job of providing the basic data, and deficiencies that exist in the data system are due to the failure of governments to obtain further critical data, such as the distribution of reserves by cost and the probable impact on known oil fields of higher prices. Thus for most minerals we have a good idea of the magnitude of economically recoverable material for which production facilities already exist. But we know very little about the cost distribution of these proved reserves and even less about the prospects for adding new reserves.

The coal resource data that are available to the public have traditionally been built on an entirely different basis from those used for other fuels. Nothing resembling the proved reserve concept exists for coal.[2] Instead, generous estimates of total resource availability based mainly on geological field surveys are employed. Whatever these figures mean, they are clearly not comparable with proved reserve figures for other fuels. Even the existence of much of this coal is uncertain, so, clearly, little can be said about economic viability. The classic error in energy analyses has been to assume that coal resource figures are comparable to those for other fuels. As a result, the potential for other fuels tends to be minimized and that for coal exaggerated. Thus the current enthusiasm over coal as the wave of the future is probably premature.[3]

With increasing government intervention in world energy markets in recent years,[4] it is very difficult to forecast future market conditions. The Organization of Petroleum Exporting Countries (OPEC) possesses the bulk of the world's *known* low-cost energy resources; its success in raising prices is one of the major causes of the re-evaluation of energy supplies in North America and elsewhere. However, until the OPEC price rose, the leading energy-consuming nations were largely content to rely on OPEC countries to meet the future growth in energy consumption.

Despite the fact that OPEC has been studied by many observers, we do not possess the analytical tools to predict, confidently, the future path of world oil prices as a result of this type of intervention.

---

[2] An excellent analysis of the drawbacks of published data on coal resources appears in Martin B. Zimmerman, "Long-Run Mineral Supply: The Case of Coal in the United States" (Ph.D. diss., Massachusetts Institute of Technology, 1975).

[3] In the early 1970s, various groups in the United States have tried to reduce this defect by developing coal reserve figures more comparable to those for other fuels; thus far the methods used to adjust the data are exceedingly rough.

[4] The discussions on these issues constitute an enormous literature. Three useful references are Edward W. Erickson and Leonard Waverman, eds., *The Energy Question, An International Failure of Policy*, 2 vols. (Toronto: University of Toronto Press, 1974); Leslie E. Grayson, ed., *Economics of Energy* (Princeton: Darwin Press, 1975); and Richard B. Mancke, *The Failure of U.S. Energy Policy* (New York: Columbia University Press, 1974).

Economists have been able to establish only that cartels have difficulties in agreeing how to share the burden of restricting output to volumes saleable at the cartel price. Some observers believe that the benefits of the OPEC agreement are so great that the cartel will persist indefinitely. Others argue that the difficulties of maintaining cohesion are so great that OPEC will inevitably collapse. Still another position is that the cartel can be made to collapse, but only if the consuming nations work together skillfully to exploit the underlying tensions by making the OPEC members so suspicious of each other that eventually one will break ranks in fear that someone else will do so first.

The problem of predicting OPEC behaviour, of course, is simply an illustration of the difficulties in predicting public policies generally. This study discusses in considerable detail the uncertainties surrounding future energy policies in the United States and Canada.

Moreover, the availability of future energy supplies will depend critically on the outcome of research and development activities that have not yet been completed (and, in some cases, may not even have been started). The estimates of the prospective costs of utilizing these new technologies are necessarily highly speculative. Unfortunately, the historical record does not inspire great confidence in such estimates, since, all too often, unexpected problems arise to inflate actual costs well above levels predicted early in the development of new technologies.

In sum, the main thing to note is that the future is enormously uncertain and all judgments should be considered highly tentative. Whether a major shift to coal will occur in the 1975-90 period depends critically upon the persistence of the high cost of oil to consumers. Such persistence could occur either because OPEC remains strong or because its collapse is offset by high trade barriers on oil imports. (Such barriers might arise because of fears of the political consequences of dependence on heavy imports of OPEC oil or to protect expensive domestic energy industries that had been established in expectation of continued high OPEC prices.) It is clear from studies by Professor M. A. Adelman that supplies of Middle East oil adequate to meet world energy demands will be physically available at production costs well below those for alternative fuels such as synthetics from coal, at least until 1985.[5] Indeed, subsequent

---

[5] Adelman's main writing on the subject is *The World Petroleum Market* (Baltimore: Johns Hopkins University Press for Resources for the Future, 1972). Two later useful discussions are "Is the Oil Shortage Real? Oil Companies As Tax Collectors" (*Foreign Policy*, No. 9 [Winter, 1972-73], pp. 69-107) and "Politics, Economics and World Oil" (*American Economic Review* 62, No. 2 [May, 1974], pp. 58-67). Examples of former critics who seem to have accepted the Adelman view on resource availability are James E. Akins, "The Oil Crisis: This Time the Wolf Is Here," *Foreign Affairs* 51, No. 3 (April, 1973), pp. 462-90, and James W. McKie, "The Political

(Cont'd on page 6)

discoveries and reduced demand resulting from higher oil prices have made the prospect of severe depletion of Middle East resources unlikely until well into the 1990s.

Even if OPEC oil remains expensive, there are other alternatives to coal, but all of them are very much more costly than existing resources. In North America, we can expand conventional oil and gas resources and develop energy from uranium, oil shale, and tar sands in the remainder of the twentieth century. Other sources may subsequently be developed. It is thus extremely difficult to be sure what pattern of energy development will occur. Particular note may be taken of the great uncertainties that past and present public policies in the United States have created about conventional supplies of oil and gas. Such practices as regulation of gas prices and hesitation over building the TransAlaska Pipeline and leasing potential oil- and gas-bearing sites on the Outer Continental Shelf have restrained the development of oil and gas supplies in the United States. Comparable restraints have been imposed by such Canadian policies as domestic price controls, shifts in resource taxation, export limitations, and delay in approving the Mackenzie Valley gasline.

Synopsis

Chapter 2 gives an overview of the past and prospective role of coal in the U.S. and Canadian energy economies. A short review of energy consumption experience and patterns of U.S.-Canadian coal trade is provided. Then forecasts, particularly those made since the massive increases in oil prices in 1973 and 1974, of energy consumption are briefly summarized.

In Chapter 3, U.S. and Canadian public policies affecting coal production and use are examined. While most of the discussion stresses environmental issues, taxation and public attitudes towards ownership patterns are also examined.

Chapter 4 discusses the comparative economics of Canadian and U.S. coal. In the opening section I examine the available data on reserves in both countries and then move on to estimate long-run supply costs under various assumptions, including those dealing with transportation costs.

In Chapter 5, I examine alternative demand patterns for coal and its synthetic-fuel derivatives. Here both the type of user (e.g., industrial, residential, and commercial) and the form in which coal

---

(Cont'd from page 5)

Economy of World Petroleum," *American Economic Review* 64, No. 2 (May, 1974), pp. 51-57. The *Petroleum Economist* (Vol. 62, No. 10, October, 1975, pp. 369-71) reports a study that supports the view that Middle East reserves can continue expanding at least until 1995. The Adelman *Foreign Policy* paper and the Akins paper are reprinted in Grayson, *op. cit.*

is consumed must be carefully integrated to form a consistent view of the long-run demand outlook. The analysis becomes more complicated because, in many instances, there is a choice of employing coal directly or using it indirectly to generate electricity or even to transform it into a synthetic fuel.

The concluding chapter synthesizes these diverse but related elements into an assessment of the changing market for coal and the potential impact on Canada-U.S. energy relations.

2

Coal and the Energy Economy: History and Prospects

There has been a persistent worldwide decline over the past three decades in the importance of coal as a basic source of energy. This decline is clearly evident in both Canada and the United States (see Table 1), where the relative position of coal in total energy consumption has dropped dramatically since the end of World War II and where even the absolute level of coal consumption had yet to recover to its former peak levels by 1974.[1]

The long-term shift away from coal in world energy markets reflects the fact that coal has been unable to compete successfully with other conventional fuels, especially oil and gas. One of the more obvious reasons for this competitive disadvantage lies in the fact that other fuels became cheaper than certain coals — e.g., those mined in Western Europe — and that, over a period of two decades or more, former coal users were able to make the switch to cheaper fuels with a minimum of cost and disruption. But elsewhere, and particularly in the United States, relative price movements were only part of the process stimulating the shift away from coal. A further influence was that costs other than direct payments for the fuel were generally considerably higher for coal than for other fuels.

---

[1] In 1974, U.S. total consumption of coal, on a BTU basis, was 83 percent of the 1947 level, but because of the shift to a lower BTU content, the actual tonnage used in 1974 was 93 percent of the 1947 consumption. Bituminous coal and lignite tonnage was actually slightly above that of 1947 but provided only 89 percent of the BTUs secured from this same coal source in 1947. Finally, anthracite production shrank drastically over the same time period (see Walter G. Dupree, Jr., and James A. West, *United States Energy Through the Year 2000* [Washington: U.S. Government Printing Office, 1972], and 1974 press release from the U.S. Bureau of Mines). In Canada the picture is similar to that of the United States. Coal consumption in 1945 equalled 1.1 quadrillion BTUs, only to decline to 0.7 quadrillion BTUs, or about 60 percent of the 1945 level, by 1974 (see Department of Energy, Mines and Resources, *An Energy Policy for Canada — Phase I*, Vol. 1 [Ottawa: Information Canada, 1973], p. 32, and unpublished data provided by the Department).

TABLE 1

**Relative Role of Coal in U.S. and Canadian Energy Consumption,
Selected Years, 1945-74**
(percentage of total energy consumed on a BTU basis)

Year	United States	Canada
1945	n.a.	51.5
1947	47.9	51.7
1950	38.0	41.9
1955	29.1	28.7
1960	22.8	14.9
1965	22.3	13.2
1970	19.2	11.0
1972	17.3	10.0
1974	18.0	8.1

n.a. = not available.

Sources: United States: Walter G. Dupree, Jr., and James A. West, *United States Energy Through the Year 2000* (Washington: U.S. Government Printing Office, 1972), and U.S. Bureau of Mines, Press Releases.
Canada: Department of Energy, Mines and Resources, *An Energy Policy for Canada — Phase I*, Vol. 1 (Ottawa: Information Canada, 1973), p. 32; data for 1974 supplied by Department of Energy, Mines and Resources.

Coal is more expensive to transport and handle by the user, requires more expensive boilers for combustion, and involves an ash-disposal problem. When these extra costs were considered in conjunction with the basic fuel costs themselves, most energy consumers decided that oil and natural gas were cheaper to use than coal.

The principal exceptions to this rule have been large-scale users of primary energy inputs, notably electric utilities, located in reasonable proximity to coal fields. The cost of coal used per additional unit of output steadily diminishes as the volume of electricity generated expands, largely because there are economies of scale in the transporting, receiving, and handling of bulk coal. Bearing this in mind, plus the fact that the demand for electricity has grown rapidly in the postwar era, it is easy to understand why there has been an ever increasing proportion of U.S. coal devoted to electricity generation. Table 2 documents this fact readily, revealing that U.S. utilities currently account for two-thirds of total U.S. coal consumption. In Canada the picture is very much the same, with 62 percent of all coal used going towards fueling electrical utilities.[2]

In only one use — the production of coke for pig iron manufacture — does coal possess special advantages in competition with other fuel sources. Despite numerous efforts to find economically preferable alternatives, coke has historically proven indispensable in

[2] See Statistics Canada, *Detailed Energy Supply and Demand* (Ottawa: Information Canada).

TABLE 2

**Relative Role of Electric Utilities and Coke Ovens
As Markets for Bituminous Coal and Lignite,
United States, Selected Years, 1947-74**
(percentage of total coal consumption)

Year	Electric Power	Coke Ovens
1947	15.8	19.2
1950	19.4	22.9
1955	33.2	25.4
1960	45.7	21.3
1965	52.9	20.6
1970	61.7	18.6
1974	70.6	16.2

Sources: Dupree and West, *op. cit.*, and U.S. Bureau of Mines, *Minerals
Yearbook* and Press Releases (based upon tonnage figures).

the manufacture of pig iron in the steel industry. Although it has
been possible to reduce substantially the amount of coke consumed
per ton of pig iron produced by such methods as greater benefication
(increasing the iron ore concentration) of iron before its use in the
blast furnace and by addition of supplemental fuels, these developments have served only to restrain growth in coke consumption.
Coke consumption in the United States over the past twenty-five
years has fluctuated considerably without showing any noticeable
growth trend.

Trade Patterns

Canada is both an exporter and an importer of coal, very much
akin to its oil position. With Canada's most attractive energy resources located in the western provinces and without substantial
facilities to transport this coal cheaply, it has not been possible for
western coal to make any significant inroads into supplying major
markets in eastern Canada. This reflects the critical role of transportation costs in the choice of fuels. On the other hand, Canadian
coal supplies are well located, relative to those of competitors, to
supply Japan. Accordingly, Canada has developed a substantial export market, principally supplying Japanese steel mills with coking
coal found in British Columbia and Alberta. In the short period
between 1968 and 1974, Canadian exports surged from 1.5 million to
12 million tons annually, with nearly all of this volume destined for
Japan.

At the same time, Canada has had to rely heavily on the United
States for imports. Of the 13.7 million tons imported from the
United States in 1974, 6 million tons went to Ontario Hydro, with

the remainder being metallurgical coal to meet the Canadian steel industry's coking needs.[3]

When the worldwide "energy crisis" broke in 1973-74, generating fears of longer-term shortages, this substantial Canadian reliance on U.S. coal became, for the first time, a source of growing concern in Canada. Many Canadians feared that Canada could no longer be assured of a continuous and adequate supply of U.S. coal for its electric utilities and its steel mills, especially in the face of growing U.S. domestic requirements and the needs of U.S. customers elsewhere in the world. For an evaluation of this view it is necessary to understand, first, the current pattern of U.S. exports and how Canada fits into this global picture.

U.S. Exports

The majority of total U.S. coal exports now go to Canada and Japan, with the great bulk of the remaining exports finding their way to various European countries. As Table 3 demonstrates, the Japanese market for U.S. coal has grown dramatically, from 147,000 tons in 1950 to a peak of just over 27,000,000 tons in 1974 — all for metallurgical purposes. Japan is almost entirely dependent on imports for its coking coal and has adopted a strategy of securing supplies from several sources. The United States and Australia are by far the largest suppliers, with their relative positions fluctuating somewhat from year to year. The Canadian exports noted earlier constitute the only really major additional supplies going to Japan, although small amounts are imported from several other countries.

TABLE 3

Pattern of U.S. Coal Exports,
Selected Years, 1950-74
(thousand tons)

Year	Total Exports	Exports to			
		Canada	Europe	Japan	Rest of World
1950	25,468	23,009	794	147	1,518
1955	51,277	17,185	28,677	2,760	2,655
1960	36,541	11,639	16,948	5,617	2,337
1965	50,181	15,661	24,957	7,491	2,072
1970	70,944	18,673	21,504	27,636	3,131
1974	59,926	13,706	15,855	27,346	3,019

Source: U.S. Bureau of Mines, *Minerals Yearbook*, various issues.

---

[3] U.S. Bureau of Mines, *Mineral Yearbook*, 1974.

European imports from the United States are predominantly of metallurgical coal and basically constitute an important, but carefully limited, supplement to domestic supplies and imports from elsewhere. The European coal industry is high-cost, necessitating heavy subsidization and protection in four of the largest industrial countries in Western Europe (Great Britain, France, Germany, and Belgium). For various reasons, most notably the resistance of major energy-consuming industries to a requirement to purchase high-cost European coals, Western Europe has been forced to allow a steady but usually carefully controlled inflow of U.S. coal. However, since the European coal industry is extremely inflexible, surges in demand for coal periodically produce surges in imports; as a result, the European market is notably less stable than those of Japan and Canada.

Canadian Imports

Canada, unlike most other markets for U.S. coal, imports both metallurgical and steam coal in significant quantities. As Table 4 indicates, Canada (mainly Ontario Hydro) represents a very important market for U.S. steam coal, one that has grown quite rapidly in the last decade and now constitutes 75 percent of all U.S. steam coal exports. In the case of metallurgical coal exports, Canada represents a smaller market; approximately 15 percent of total U.S. metallurgical exports are absorbed by Canada. Thus Canada is an important but not a dominant market for U.S. coal exporters, and, in fact, trails both Europe and Japan in recent years. However, from Canada's point of view, imports from the United States are essentially the only economically viable source of coal for Canada's steel industry and for Ontario Hydro.

TABLE 4

**Canadian Market for U.S. Coal,
Selected Years, 1962-74**

Year	U.S. Metallurgical Coal Exports to Canada As Percentage of Total U.S. Metallurgical Coal Exports	U.S. Steam Coal Exports to Canada As Percentage of Total U.S. Steam Coal Exports
1962	21.2	42.5
1965	18.8	53.1
1969	15.1	71.9
1972	17.0	72.0
1974	14.5	75.3

Source: U.S. Bureau of Mines, *International Coal Trade*, various issues.

In view of these facts, many Canadians have felt concern over a possible loss or limitation of U.S. exports of coal. If the United

States were to restrict coal exports, would Canada necessarily be exempted? Would Canadian steel mills and Ontario Hydro be able to obtain their requirements in the event of a U.S. embargo, imposed because of an anticipated growth of U.S. domestic demand over the next decade or so?

Of course, care should be taken not to exaggerate the dangers to Canada's position. Canada could shift to Japan much of the burden of the loss of its metallurgical coal supplies by imposing a coal-export embargo of its own, and Ontario Hydro might be able to convert to oil or gas. These adjustments would not be easy, but it is not clear that they would be more difficult than the adjustments that would be required by other consumers of U.S. coal.

The remainder of this study examines important bilateral issues in coal trade arising out of Canada's dependency on the United States. To begin the analysis, we turn to an appraisal of prospective developments in the metallurgical and steam coal markets in the United States. Briefly, the main concerns to date have been related to strains on metallurgical coal supplies resulting from depletion, growing domestic and foreign steel industry demands, and the potential use of metallurgical-quality coal for steam generation because of its low sulfur content.

Demand Outlook

The sharp rises in oil prices since late 1973 have already de-stroyed the relevance of just about every earlier forecast of energy prospects for the long run. The higher prices will lower total energy consumption and change the roles of different fuels in a fashion that is extremely difficult to predict at this time. Several forecasts have appeared suggesting how energy consumption and its distribution among the various alternative fuels might change through 1985, but few forecasts to the year 2000 are available.

Many different views exist about the overall impact of higher energy prices, the policy responses they will produce, and the implications for coal. Table 5 is designed to give some flavour of the wide range of views on U.S. coal prospects before and after the 1973-74 rises in oil costs. First, the projections from two 1972 re-ports are shown. The first study, which extends to the year 2000, was produced by Dupree and West of the U.S. Department of the Interior staff; the second, covering only the period to 1985, was prepared by the National Petroleum Council (NPC), an industry advisory group to the Department of the Interior. The NPC, as shown, explored various possible total energy demand levels — two of which are higher than those expected by Dupree and West.

Similarly, the results of two 1974 forecasts — the Project Inde-pendence Blueprint (PIB) and the report of the Energy Policy Project funded by the Ford Foundation — are shown. These are supple-

TABLE 5

Comparative Forecasts of Coal and Total Energy Consumption, United States, 1985 and 2000

A. *Forecasts for 1985*

Source and Model	Oil Price	Supply Posture	Special Conservation Measures	Coal (million tons)	Coal (quadrillion BTUs)	Total Energy (quadrillion BTUs)	Coal As Percentage of Total
Dupree and West (1972)				893	21.47	116.63	18.4
National Petroleum Council (1972):[a]							
High				1,570	27.10	130.0	20.8
Intermediate				1,134	21.39	124.9	17.1
Low				1,004	20.30	112.5	18.0
Project Independence (1974):							
	$ 7	As usual	No	865.45	19.89	109.06	18.2
	$ 7	As usual	Yes	712.90	16.72	99.18	16.9
	$ 7	Accelerated	No	762.11	17.73	109.55	16.2
	$ 7	Accelerated	Yes	635.28	15.18	99.66	15.2
	$11	As usual	No	1,005.14	22.86	102.92	22.2
	$11	As usual	Yes	850.08	19.67	94.16	20.9
	$11	Accelerated	No	918.02	21.06	104.18	20.2
	$11	Accelerated	Yes	700.23	16.44	96.25	17.1
Energy Policy Project (1974):							
Historical growth:							
Domestic oil and gas				n.a.	28	116.1	24.1
High nuclear				n.a.	26	116.1	22.4
High imports				n.a.	21	116.1	18.1
Technical fix:							
Self-sufficiency				n.a.	16	91.3	17.5
Environmental protection				n.a.	14	91.3	15.3
Zero energy growth				n.a.	14	88.1	15.9
ERDA scenarios (1975):[b]							
(0) No new initiatives				1,006	21.14	107.30	19.7
(1) Improved end-use efficiency				879	18.46	96.97	19.0
(2) Emphasis on synthetic fuels				1,108	23.28	107.28	21.7
(3) Emphasis on electrification				957	20.10	106.77	18.8
(4) Limited nuclear				951	19.98	107.05	18.7
(5) Combination of strategies of scenarios 1, 2, and 3				863	18.13	98.14	18.5

B. Forecasts for 2000

Source and Model	Coal (million tons)	Coal (quadrillion BTUs)	Total Energy (quadrillion BTUs)	Coal As Percentage of Total
Dupree and West (1972)	1,310	31.36	191.90	16.3
Energy Policy Project (1974):				
Historical growth:				
Domestic oil and gas	n.a.	44	186.7	23.6
High nuclear	n.a.	45	186.7	24.1
High imports	n.a.	47	186.7	25.2
Technical fix:				
Self-sufficiency	n.a.	28	124.0	22.6
Environmental protection	n.a.	26	124.0	21.0
Zero energy growth	n.a.	18	100.0	18.0
ERDA scenarios (1975):[b]				
(0) No new initiatives	1,614	33.89	165.47	20.5
(1) Improved end-use efficiency	1,091	22.91	122.48	18.7
(2) Emphasis on synthetic fuels	2,370	49.77	165.42	30.1
(3) Emphasis on electrification	1,453	30.51	161.16	18.9
(4) Limited nuclear	2,184	45.87	158.01	29.0
(5) Combination of strategies of scenarios 1, 2, and 3	1,862	39.11	137.03	28.5

n.a. = not available.

[a] NPC coal figures relate to maximum availability and not to prospective consumption.

[b] The ERDA figures include exports.

Sources: Dupree and West, *op. cit.*; National Petroleum Council, *U.S. Energy Outlook* (Washington, 1972); U.S. Federal Energy Administration, *Project Independence Report* (Washington: U.S. Government Printing Office, 1974); Energy Policy Project of the Ford Foundation, *A Time to Choose: America's Energy Future* (Cambridge, Mass.: Ballinger Publishing Company, 1974); and U.S. Energy Research and Development Administration, *A National Plan for Energy Research, Development and Demonstration: Creating Energy Choice for the Future*, Vol. 1, *The Plan* (Washington, 1975).

mented by data from a series of demand and supply scenarios that the Energy Research and Development Administration (ERDA) prepared in 1975.

The Project Independence projections, which extend only to 1985, developed eight cases. Each case involves a different combination of assumptions about the three key influences — whether oil prices are $7 or $11 per barrel, whether supply is "business as usual" or "accelerated development," and whether or not special conservation measures are employed. In practice, "as usual" actually assumes a modest reduction of existing impediments to production, and "acceleration" means even greater stimulus. The meaning of the presence or absence of conservation is not clear; apparently, conservation consists of extra reductions of energy use produced by eliminating public policies that cause inefficient energy consumption and by educating consumers about profitable ways to reduce fuel use.

The Energy Policy Project has three basic demand scenarios — historical growth (essentially a measure of what demand would have been had prices not risen), "technical fix" (roughly assuming a response to higher prices combined with more stringent environmental and conservation measures than in Project Independence), and zero growth (the imposition of policies stringent enough to produce an eventual drop in the energy growth rate to zero). The first two cases have subcases involving different supply mixes determined by the choice of policies. Thus the technical-fix self-sufficiency subcase allows for more oil and gas imports than the environmental protection subcase because such imports are felt to have a lower environmental impact.

The ERDA scenario seems to have been designed to show what is technologically possible rather than what is economically feasible and sensible. In many respects, ERDA's expectations concerning total energy use in 1985 reflect views similar to those implied in the Project Independence model, but ERDA's scenarios also imply a higher level of energy consumption in the year 2000 than is forecast in the Energy Policy Project's technical-fix case. Moreover, the strategies examined by ERDA are predominantly designed to encourage greater coal use; thus by the year 2000, when sufficient time has elapsed in which to implement the required policies, coal consumption is generally well above the Dupree and West forecasts. Several additional forecasts exist; however, an examination of these estimates would not materially alter the outlook for coal.

Without attempting an exhaustive review of the forecasts, a quick inspection should suggest that, by and large, the 1974 projections assume that the net effect of higher energy prices is to reduce coal consumption, particularly for 1985, below the levels assumed in the 1972 forecasts. With the Project Independence cases, the main reason for the generally lower forecasts of coal consumption is the optimism about the future importance of nuclear power (which the very recent delays and cancellations probably have made unrealistic, at least for 1985). Overall, the Energy Policy Project predicts lower coal use because it projects sharply lower energy consumption than do the other studies. Only the ERDA scenarios assuming high coal use lead to markedly higher coal consumption projections.

Turning to the outlook for coal in Canada, the most recent report of the Department of Energy, Mines and Resources projects substantial increases in the demand for coal to 1990.[4] Table 6 summarizes the Department's official estimates, which employ a number of assumptions regarding the future course of energy prices and economic activity. Surprisingly, although coal consumption is expected to grow annually between 5 and 6 percent to 1990 — well above the anticipated growth rate for total energy consumption — coal's share of Canada's total energy needs is not expected to increase above its current level. Thus even under the most favourable energy-price and economic-growth conditions in Canada, coal is expected to face stiff competition from alternative energy sources.

TABLE 6

**Forecast of Coal and Total Energy Demand,
Canada, 1976-90**
(annual average percentage change)

| | High-Price Scenario[a] | | Low-Price Scenario[b] | |
Economic Growth:	High[c]	Low[d]	High[c]	Low[d]
Total Energy:				
1976-80	4.5	4.5	5.1	5.1
1981-90	4.3	3.2	4.7	3.6
1976-90	4.3	3.7	4.8	4.1
Coal:				
1976-80	7.3	7.3	7.8	7.8
1981-90	5.2	4.0	5.7	4.5
1976-90	5.9	5.1	6.4	5.6

[a] Assumes that domestic oil prices increase relatively faster than the general price level and reach $13 per barrel, in 1975 dollars, by 1978. Prices for electricity and coal are assumed to increase accordingly, and the price of natural gas is again assumed to reach "commodity-equivalent" value with oil by the late 1970s. After 1978, all energy prices are assumed to increase at only the general rate of inflation.
[b] Assumes that the domestic price of oil remains constant, in 1975 dollars, throughout the period; that the price of natural gas moves to "commodity-equivalent" value with oil in the latter part of the 1970s; and that the prices for electricity and coal also remain constant in real terms.
[c] Assumes potential economic growth of 5.2 percent annually in the 1980s.
[d] Assumes potential economic growth of 3.6 percent annually in the 1980s.
Source: Energy, Mines and Resources Canada, *An Energy Strategy for Canada: Policies for Self-Reliance* (Ottawa: Supply and Services, 1976), Chap. 2.

---

[4] *An Energy Strategy for Canada: Policies for Self-Reliance* (Ottawa: Supply and Services Canada, 1976), Chap. 2.

In short, the outlook calls for an increase in coal consumption over the next two or three decades, but there is little agreement as to either the timing or the dimensions of the change in the pattern of energy use. Even more unsettling is the fact that some respectable forecasts do not call for any marked increase in the use of coal relative to other energy forms. Is the widespread confidence now placed in coal as the energy saviour of the future seriously misplaced? For some insight into the answer to this question, we must turn to the next three chapters, which review the forces affecting the supply and demand for coal in the longer run.

3

Role of Public Policy in Coal Development

With coal entering a new era, featuring rising prices for oil and gas, a considerable controversy has erupted over the numerous regulatory measures governing critical phases in the production and consumption of coal. On the production side, existing government regulations not only threaten to impose severe restraints on the current U.S. ability to extract coal, but also raise major doubts about coal's ability to meet longer-run energy requirements. Similarly, the demand for coal is being directly influenced by government policy in ways that tend to jeopardize coal's future as a major alternative to domestic oil and gas supplies. Moreover, the rash of government regulations introduced over the past five or more years have created a good deal of uncertainty and have also raised the possibility of further, and perhaps even radical, policy changes bearing directly on long-range supply and demand in the coal industry. Although considerable controversy exists about the reasonableness of existing and proposed government policies affecting coal, it is widely conceded that effective business planning is nearly impossible without some clear guidelines.

Coal policies appropriate to domestic energy goals have not emerged and are unlikely to emerge in the near future. Despite this weakness in policy direction, both countries have taken some initiatives in the area of coal; however, this chapter has far more to say about U.S. than about Canadian policies. This weighting reflects the greater complexity of existing U.S. policy problems and the fact that Canada has not formulated policies in some key areas.

U.S. Policies

In the United States, several basic policies affecting coal production can be distinguished:[1]

---

[1] This list by no means exhausts the policy issues relating to coal in the United States. All phases of the coal process, from mining to ultimate use, involve some degree of concern with air- and water-pollution problems. At one time, for example, extensive concern existed about the leaching of acid material from a coal seam by passing water through mines and then discharging the contaminated water into

(Cont'd on page 20)

- the Federal Coal Mine Health and Safety Act, particularly as it was radically altered in 1969;
- the regulation of strip mining;
- federal policies for coal leasing; and
- sulfur-emission standards.

In the following sections, the major elements of each of these basic policies are reviewed and, where possible, evaluated in terms of their impact on the long-run production potential in the United States.

Mine Health and Safety

The Coal Mine Health and Safety Act of 1969 established elaborate procedures to improve working conditions in coal mines and to compensate victims of past practices. The complexities of the law and its amendments are too extensive to review adequately here. More critically, an interpretation is hampered by bitter controversies about the costs and benefits of the law that remain to be resolved. The following is a rough outline of the basic provisions of the law and its enforcement:

- Identification of a wide number of areas (e.g., dust levels, their measurement and control, roof support, ventilation, electrical equipment, fire protection, explosives, and communications) in which practices were to be improved to lessen health and safety hazards.
- Establishment of a program to check on lung damage to miners and to provide compensation for the health effects.
- A major increase in the frequency and severity of coal mine inspections.
- Increased research on safer or healthier methods of mining.
- Improved training programs to ensure better practices in mines.

The clearly uncontroversial conclusions that can be reached about the act are that it mandated safety activities that required extra manpower and it increased outlays in safety equipment. All these factors have raised costs, and the extra tasks required have resulted in a once-and-for-all drop in the level of output per worker. Beyond this, acrimonious debates have arisen over the effects of the act. The United Mine Workers have often complained that the act is inadequately enforced. Some coal industry sources contend that the act and its enforcement have had devastating effects on the viability of the industry (implicitly arguing that the costs of the act have not brought commensurate benefits). Complaints are directed at the rules themselves, which are considered to impose not only immediate costs but barriers to technical progress and future pro-

(Cont'd from page 19)

the rivers and streams of Appalachia. While control of this problem has been required, discussion of the subject now appears only in highly specialized documents, such as the technical reports of the U.S. Environmental Protection Agency.

ductivity gains. It is also argued that the frequent visits of newly hired inspectors who lack adequate training and are often former miners with grudges against the industry caused severe interference with production.

The validity of these complaints has never been the subject of extensive impartial review. We cannot be sure how many cost increases the act produced, to what extent these impacts were transitory, and whether the costs were justified by the benefits. What is known is that output per man-day in underground mining declined about 30 percent from 1969 to 1974 (with the bulk of the decline from 1969 to 1971), and no signs of a major reversal have yet emerged. However, the Coal Mine Health and Safety Act was not the only factor affecting coal mine costs (see Chapter 4), and even before the act was passed, some observers of the coal industry feared that advances in output per worker would be much slower in the 1970s than they had been in the prior two decades.[2]

Strip-Mining Concerns

The environmental impacts of strip-mining — the removal of coal by first uncovering the overlying material and then extracting by use of earth-moving equipment — have been under attack for many years. Strip-mining without reclamation can produce land disturbance that residents of, and visitors to, the area find highly objectionable and that precludes agricultural or recreational use of the land. The pits can be safety hazards, and rainwater washing through the mine can deposit silt and acidic material in waterways. These problems are a graphic example of what discussions of environmental issues refer to as the "site-specific" characteristics of the situation — i.e., that each case involves different risks and must be judged on an individual basis.

In particular, quite distinct problems arise in the Appalachian region outside Ohio, in Ohio and the Middle West, and west of the Mississippi. The nature of strip-mining and its damage is naturally

---

[2] Little systematic analytical discussion of the law, its administration, and its effects seems to exist. The summary here draws factual information from various issues of *Coal Age*, especially the March, 1970, issue, which contained an extensive descriptive review of the law. The evaluations have been gleaned from reading *Coal Age* and other publications devoted to coal mining and from discussions with those within or close to the industry. The fears about technical progress centred on the problem that the main source of increased output per man-day in underground mines — the introduction of continuous-mining machines that cut and loaded coal in one operation — had proceeded as far as possible. Indeed, the machines could remove coal far more rapidly than it could be transported from the seam to the surface, and the need for faster haulage methods was seen as critical. Some observers felt that the Health and Safety Act would impede development of such improvements, but Consolidation Coal Company has been experimenting with a system that adapts the technique of pipelining coal in a slurry form that has been used for long-distance hauling for underground use.

quite different when the cover is hilly, as in most of Appalachia, than when it is flat. Mining conditions and restoration of the land are both more difficult in such hilly land. However, a different complication occurs west of the Mississippi: the aridity of the land is such that revegetation can be extremely expensive.

Strip-mining is regulated by state laws of varying stringency, but efforts to pass a federal law have proved unsuccessful. After several years of discussion, a bill passed Congress in 1974, only to be successfully vetoed by President Ford; a similar fate met a 1975 bill. As of early 1976, no active efforts were under way to develop a new strip-mining bill, although several unsuccessful attempts had been made to amend other energy legislation to incorporate the vetoed bill.[3]

Land-Leasing Policies

Western coal development is profoundly influenced by the dominant role of the U.S. government as the principal owner of coal-bearing land (or at least the mineral rights to such land). This control implies that the U.S. government has a major impact on how much coal land is made available and the terms under which the coal may be exploited. Moreover, the requirement of Environmental Impact Statements has complicated the process of federal leasing. Statements are required for the leasing program as a whole, for leasing in individual areas, and for the use of federal lands for whatever might be associated with the coal mining (e.g., an electric-power or synthetic-fuel plant, power lines, rail spurs, or pipelines).

In designing a leasing program, both the direct effects on the market behaviour of the coal industry and the environmental effects must be considered. The latter issue includes developing a strip-mine reclamation policy for federal lands. In addition, considerable concern exists not only over the disturbance of land but over the influx of large numbers of people into a sparsely settled region, and a leasing policy must assuage these concerns. The economic impacts involve both the vigour of competition and the sharing of profits. Fears have been expressed that control of coal will accumulate in the hands of a few companies and that they will collude to control prices. It is further argued that if these landowners are oil companies, their collusion will be designed to limit competition between coal and conventional sources of oil and gas. Thus the fear is that coal will be developed too slowly and in too limited amounts.

---

[3] The literature on strip-mine reclamation is enormous and continually growing. Two documents prepared for the U.S. Senate Committee on Interior and Insular Affairs — a 1971 collection of readings, *The Issues Relating to Surface Mining*, and a 1973 study, *Coal Surface Mining and Reclamation*, conducted by the Council on Environmental Quality — should provide more than sufficient information for the average reader.

Critics of this argument note that, given the large number of oil companies and others interested in western coal and the comparatively simple technologies involved in strip-mining, a coal monopoly seems unlikely. Support for this view has been provided by the rapid new entry of firms not previously producing oil or coal, such as Utah International and the Pacific Power and Light-Kiewit group, into large-scale production.

The profit-sharing issue is a classic problem in mineral policy-making. The basic source of the difficulties arises from the economic heterogeneity of mineral deposits. Variations in quality of the mineral contained and differences in the ease of mining and transporting the material to market create major differences in competitive position. Thus for any given mineral one can define a hierarchy of deposits according to their relative attractiveness in terms of costs and profitability (a phenomenon crudely represented in every elementary economics textbook by the upward-sloping supply curve). For the industry as a whole, the market price that equates overall supply and demand is usually determined by cost conditions prevailing in the least profitable mining site.[4] Consequently, if the market price rises to make less-profitable deposits viable, then all those more profitable mines with richer ("intramarginal") deposits will be earning what economists refer to as "economic rents" — i.e., a rate of profit greater than the acceptable minimum needed to justify the creation and maintenance of the operation. There is a widely held philosophy that these "rents" should be taken away from the mine or landowner and transferred to the general public, since they arise from lucky access to bounty created by nature, rather than from superior skills or technology.[5]

Unfortunately, while the basic principle is widely accepted, its implementation involves many problems. The definition of the appropriate "public" and how to reward it are often causes of considerable dispute. In particular, a basic question arises about the extent to which the region in which mining occurs deserves special consideration. To the extent that such local claims are accepted, a choice exists between surrender of the authority to capture the economic rents to the region and retention of this power by the federal government combined with transfer of its receipts to the states. Moreover, complex technical problems arise in imposing a system of collecting the rents in a fashion that meets all the goals that are generally defined. Such goals include securing all the rents, avoiding distortion of output, administrative simplicity, and allow-

---

[4] In technical terms, market equilibrium occurs at a price at which the quantity produced equals the quantity demanded, and this price is sufficient to ensure the profitability of the economically-least-attractive deposit in use.

[5] Note that whether the transfer is called a royalty, lease payment, tax, or whatever is a purely legal distinction; what counts economically is the form the payment takes.

ing wide access to the land to a sufficient number of producers to prevent monopoly. A rich literature shows that these objectives are often in conflict. For example, a simple tax, such as a uniform sales tax, fails to tax the more profitable ventures more severely.[6]

Largely because of the series of Environmental Impact Statements that must be prepared, formulation of a leasing policy has proved quite difficult. For example, well over a year (i.e., far more than the legally required period) elapsed between the issue of a draft and the final Environmental Impact Statement on coal leasing.[7] The final statement immediately produced complaints from the head of the Environmental Protection Agency that the proposed reclamation policy was inadequate, and several environmental groups threatened to institute law suits opposing the proposed program. Congress may intervene by legislation to alter the leasing policy. Thus considerable uncertainty prevails over what U.S policy towards coal mining will be.

Problem of Sulfur Emissions

The primary influence on coal use in the United States, for reasons noted in Chapter 5, is regulations affecting the emission of sulfur oxides — principally by electric-power plants. As with controls on coal production, the regulatory system here is extremely complex. Basic federal policy has three elements — air quality standards, specific-source emission standards, and the principle of no significant degradation.

In simple terms, air quality standards govern the overall concentration of pollutants in the air, while emission standards restrict the rate of pollution from an individual source. The non-degradation rule states that regions with air quality now significantly better than the federal standard cannot let air quality decline to the upper limit set by federal standards. The federal air quality standards and the specific-source rules are set on entirely different bases (with no guarantee that consistent results are produced).

---

[6] Two excellent discussions of the problems of collecting economic rents may be found in Henry Steele, "Natural Resource Taxation: Resource Allocation and Distribution Implications," in Mason Gaffney, ed., *Extractive Resources and Taxation* (Madison: University of Wisconsin Press, 1967), pp. 233-67, and Walter Mead, "Federal Public Lands Leasing Policy," *Quarterly of the Colorado School of Mines* 64, No. 4 (October, 1969), pp. 181-214.

[7] The *Draft Environmental Impact Statement: Proposed Federal Coal Leasing Program* is undated; the *Final Environmental Impact Statement: Proposed Federal Coal Leasing Program* indicates (pp. 1-3) that the draft was issued in May, 1974. The final report was released September 19, 1975. Both statements were prepared by the Bureau of Land Management of the U.S. Department of the Interior: the Bureau published the draft, and the U.S. Government Printing Office the final report. Independently of the argument over this report, a suit against the Interior Department is already under way.

Air quality standards are intended to ensure that overall levels of pollution are kept within safe limits. Primary standards that were supposed to become effective in July, 1975, are set to eliminate hazards to human health, and more stringent secondary standards are set to eliminate other effects, such as harm to property and vegetation. However, there was considerable difficulty in attaining widespread compliance with these standards, and the implementation process has been delayed.

Federal specific-source emission standards, in contrast, are based on what the U.S. Environmental Protection Agency (EPA) judges to be technically feasible levels of control. Such specific-source rules apply only to facilities that entered into construction after the regulations were issued. Depending upon the concentration of these specific sources in a particular region, it is conceivable that controls upon them would produce greater or lesser improvement in air quality than is required to meet the basic standards. (State standards for specific sources, however, presumably are tailored specifically to meet the air quality standards.)

To complicate matters further, air quality standards are met by plans designed by the individual states. The federal air quality standards, moreover, are only upper limits on the states, which can choose to opt for cleaner air than required by EPA.

In any case, widely varying sulfur-emission rules apply to different users of coal. The EPA specific-source standard implies that 0.6 pounds of sulfur may be emitted for each million BTUs used by a new electric steam-generating plant (coming into service around 1976). In equivalent terms, this would mean burning 24 million BTUs per ton of coal with 0.8 percent sulfur by weight content or 16 million BTUs per ton of coal with 0.5 percent sulfur by weight content.

Situations can exist where a given plant has to meet either much more or much less stringent rules. An older plant in a sufficiently sparsely settled area might burn a higher-sulfur coal while still meeting the air quality standards. Conversely, in an area of dense concentration of facilities, a determination by a state to impose stricter standards than those of EPA could lead to emission rules stricter than the EPA new-plant standard. A combination of the first two situations has produced stricter standards in major urban areas such as metropolitan New York and Los Angeles. A desire to prevent degradation arose in many western states even before the concept was defined by the courts. This has produced an interesting anomaly for coal produced west of the Mississippi. When shipped east of the Mississippi, it often can be burned without use of special sulfur-pollution-control devices. However, in states where coal is mined, concern over degradation has produced pressure to install such control devices.[8]

In summary, a wide range of sulfur regulations prevail in the United States. Several difficulties involved in attaining compliance have produced pressures to delay or revise sulfur-pollution standards. Thus far, only limited delays have been explicitly allowed by air-pollution agencies. Court orders have, however, been issued to delay enforcement of the rules on the ground that satisfactory compliance technology does not exist.

The other major use of coal — coke manufacture — also involves air-pollution and occupational-safety problems. Both the charging and the discharging of the coke ovens involve release of pollutants that severely affect coke-oven workers and the surrounding population in general. This problem has thus far not had major impacts on coal use; conceivably, the combination of the development of better ways of operating existing ovens and the development of new, less-pollution-prone coking technologies can prevent problems from arising.

In general, U.S. policy has created considerable difficulties for coal production and consumption. Later chapters seek to evaluate the impacts of these policies upon the competitive cost position of coal.

Canadian Policies

As noted earlier in this chapter, much less can be said about Canadian coal policy because the problems are fewer and the policies less advanced. The same two basic issues — air pollution and how best to exploit coal resources — are of major concern.

Emission Standards

Air pollution from coal use is a problem mainly in Ontario. Canada has been doubly blessed — by fewer concentrations of economic activity in which severe pollution can develop and by the ability of water power to meet the electricity-generating needs of some provinces. Ontario is, however, heavily industrialized and, as noted, relies upon coal to produce much of its electricity. In terms of air quality standards for sulfur oxides, Ontario's rules are roughly comparable to the secondary standards of the U.S. EPA in that both call for annual average levels of 0.02 parts per million.

However, emission standards in Canada are more flexible and, for example, allow for "intermittent" controls — i.e., permit use of higher-sulfur fuels except when weather conditions inadequately

---

[8] An Environmental Protection Agency report, *State Implementation Plan Emission Regulations for Sulfur Oxides: Fuel Combustion* (Research Triangle Park, 1976), indicates that a wide range of specific standards prevail. In parts of New York and New Jersey, coal must contain less than 0.2 percent sulfur by weight. In contrast, there are regions in Illinois and Indiana in which the sulfur content can exceed 3.0 percent by weight.

disperse the pollution. Under existing public regulations some Ontario Hydro plants are permitted to burn sizable amounts of 1.7 percent sulfur coal.[9] Thus the Canadian definition of environmentally acceptable coal may prove less stringent than the EPA new-source standard because U.S. pollution problems are more severe. As a result, this standard may not have a sizable impact on Canadian coal consumption in the future.

Mining Policy

In contrast to the U.S. situation, Canadian mining policy is largely a provincial matter. Although there is a well-established coal industry in eastern Canada (Nova Scotia), future expansion of coal output is most likely to take place in Alberta, British Columbia, and Saskatchewan, where the richest deposits lie. The western provinces have yet to define coal policies, at least to the same degree as in the United States, but some early hints of possible developments have emerged. The Alberta government, for example, recently announced that in 1976 it intends to introduce a comprehensive coal policy which will deal with such issues as environmental control, conservation, and the collection of economic rents.

The question of collecting the economic rents from an enlarged coal industry could generate a number of domestic issues within the federal-provincial context. As a result of the sharp rise in world oil prices in 1973-74, a serious conflict arose between Alberta and the federal government over the sharing of royalties and other forms of taxes in the oil and gas industries. Should coal prices exhibit a similar jump in the coming years, it is entirely possible that the producing provinces and the federal government might be involved in a similar domestic quarrel over the sharing of resource taxation. Such a conflict could well hurt the potential development of the coal industry in western Canada.

The statement that mining policy towards coal is a provincial matter should be qualified in at least one respect. The federal government in Canada does have ownership claims to a limited, but not inconsequential, block of land in British Columbia — often referred to as the Dominion Coal Blocks. Recently, with the prospects for coal improving markedly, the province of British Columbia has openly disputed the federal claim to this land, and the question of its disposal remains unsettled.

Another important point of comparison between Canada and the United States is that Canada does face the potential of a comparatively rapid depletion of its low-cost reserves. This concern is greatest in Alberta, where provincial authorities have calculated that the province's known supply of cheap, strippable coal reserves could be severely depleted within a span of 75 years. Rapid depletion

---

[9] This information was obtained directly from Ontario Hydro.

is quite conceivable, given that the demand for Albertan coal not only reflects that province's future electrical-power needs, but also includes potential raw coal exports to Ontario Hydro and the exports of coal-based synthetic fuels to other parts of the country and perhaps even to the United States. According to the province's own projections, strippable reserves are sufficient, in terms of 1973 production levels, for another 878 years. However, this adequacy would evaporate quickly should all the expected provincial and export demands materialize, in which case reserves in the year 2001 would suffice to maintain production levels in that year for only 37 additional years.[10]

Interestingly, a significant controversy has arisen between the two major government bodies responsible for developing a coal policy in Alberta. The Alberta Environment Conservation Authority (AECA) recommends that only a small increase in coal production be allowed in the future; this is in sharp contrast to the view of the Alberta Energy Resources Conservation Board (AERCB), which advocates the development of the province's full reserve potential as soon as possible. The AECA contends that the province's coal deposits have been overstated by the AERCB in terms of both total and recoverable reserves.[11]

Given the potential for depletion of these lowest-cost reserves, the province wishes to ensure that the coal will be available for what it considers the most important uses — meeting local electric-power needs and providing the basis of a synthetic-fuel industry. Such an industry would start in the near future by producing ammonia and methanol, proceed to provide low-BTU gas for local use by the late seventies, and ultimately move on to production of pipeline-quality gas.[12]

Ownership Policies

Another issue that continually arises, but which to date has not greatly affected policy-making, is concern over private-ownership patterns. This issue takes somewhat different forms in the two countries. The main U.S. issue is whether an energy monopoly is emerging within the U.S. economy, a concern primarily stimulated by a series of acquisitions in the late 1960s of major coal companies by other firms — particularly oil companies. Conjecture arose as early as 1969 that the oil companies were ensuring reserves for the impending manufacture of massive amounts of synthetic fuels from

[10] See Alberta Energy Resources Conservation Board, *The Adequacy of Alberta's Reserves of Surface Mineable Subbituminous Coal to Meet Market Requirements* (Calgary, 1974).
[11] *Globe and Mail* (Toronto), March 18, 1976.
[12] This information was secured during the course of a telephone conversation with Dr. Norman Berkowitz of the Alberta Energy Conservation Board.

coal.[13] When coal prices started rising sharply in 1969, a number of observers, notably the American Public Power Association, charged that the increases were part of a conspiracy by the oil companies to effect a general rise in energy prices.[14]

At the very least, we can argue that the charges have been unsubstantiated. A more recent (1974) Federal Trade Commission (FTC) study of competition in energy concludes that while "concentration" (the percentage of the market supplied by the largest firms) has been rising, this is due almost entirely to separate increases in concentration for the individual fuels, with very little of the change resulting from diversification. The FTC concludes that the market share of the twenty largest firms in energy production would have fallen from 57 percent to 54.5 percent if the companies' coal and uranium operations were excluded. (For the top eight, the change is from 37.8 to 37.0 percent.)[15] The FTC adds that, despite the increases, "concentration is low compared to many other industries."[16]

One can go further and suggest at least four flaws in the arguments that oil company entry into the coal business has been or will be a threat to competition. The first is that the argument completely ignores the substantial differences among the characteristics of oil companies. In particular, the argument assumes that, because many of the companies in the oil industry are giants with worldwide influence and possibly some influence on price, all oil companies have this attribute. This is quite incorrect. Many oil companies, including most of those that purchased coal companies, are, in fact, relatively small factors in the oil industry. Gulf, which ranked third in 1970 U.S. oil production and sixth in 1972 refinery capacity[17] and is considered "an international major," is the only oil industry purchaser of a coal company that can be classified as a "giant." In fact, Gulf acquired its coal company as a by-product of a merger with

[13] See U.S. Federal Trade Commission, Bureau of Economics, *Economic Report on Corporate Mergers* (Washington: U.S. Government Printing Office, 1969), especially Chapter 8.
[14] A number of Congressional hearings were held on the subject; see, for example, U.S. House of Representatives, Subcommittee on Special Small Business Problems of the Select Committee on Small Business, *The Impact of the Energy and Fuel Crisis* (Washington: U.S. Government Printing Office, 1970), and *Concentration by Competing Raw Fuel Industries in the Energy Market and Its Impact on Small Business*, 2 vols. (Washington: U.S. Government Printing Office, 1971). The American Public Power Association's views can be found in both hearings. More recently, a particularly accessible and well-publicized expression of the concerns appears in the final report of the Energy Policy Project of the Ford Foundation, *A Time to Choose* (Cambridge, Mass.: Ballinger Publishing Company, 1974).
[15] Joseph P. Mulholland and Douglas W. Webbink, *Concentration Levels and Trends in the Energy Sector of the U.S. Economy*, staff report of the Federal Trade Commission (Washington: U.S. Government Printing Office, 1974), especially page 137.
[16] *Ibid.*, p. 148.
[17] Thomas D. Duchesneau, *Competition in the U.S. Energy Industry* (Cambridge, Mass: Ballinger Publishing Company, 1975), pp. 37 and 44.

Spencer Chemical, and the coal company in question ranked four-teenth in 1974 U.S. production.[18]

In contrast, Continental Oil, which "purchased" the second-largest coal producer, the Consolidation Coal Company, ranks much lower among oil companies; it had only 2.5 percent of 1972 refining capacity.[19] The other oil companies with coal production are even less important. Occidental Petroleum, which acquired the Island Creek and Maust Coal Companies (with the latter merged into the former, which ranks third in production), for example, does not even produce or refine oil in the United States.

A second consideration is that the prospects for synthetic fuel have been so uncertain and involve so long a lead time that obtaining coal for this purpose could not have weighed heavily in the decision to acquire operating coal companies; the current intrinsic profitability of existing mines would have been the critical consideration. The purchases were mainly of going operations; if the need was for reserves, direct acquisition of reserves would have been a more logical strategy.

A third point is that there are simpler, more easily documented explanations of the coal price increase — namely, rising costs and unanticipated demand increases that strained capacity. The cost-increase issue is reviewed in Chapter 4, although that discussion omits a review of the capacity strains of 1969 and 1974 that caused spot prices to soar above costs, so I comment on that aspect of the problem here. The 1969 developments are generally attributed to, among other things, tightness in the world tanker market owing to various factors, such as the curtailment of oil production in Libya and the closing of the Suez Canal and the pipeline from Saudi Arabia to the Mediterranean, all of which meant that longer oil hauls were necessary. In addition, delays arose in the construction of nuclear plants. All these forces caused a surge in demand for the limited portion of coal output not committed under long-term contracts. A similar surge arose in the wake of the Arab oil boycott of 1973-74.[20]

Finally, fears that purchases of reserves by coal companies bode ill for future competition in the coal industry seem to reflect a

---

[18] See Duchesneau on the history of the merger and *Coal Age*, April, 1975, p. 40, for data on the ranking of the leading coal producers.

[19] Duchesneau, *op. cit.*, p. 44. The quotation marks around the word purchase are to indicate that the merger may have been designed to take advantage of a tax gimmick, subsequently abolished, that allowed Continental to obtain the money to buy Consolidation at a low effective cost.

[20] In a widely publicized discussion of this issue, the U.S. Council on Wage and Price Stability accepts the view that demand forces were probably the true cause of price increases. However, in its report the Council relies heavily on published evaluations of competition in the coal industry, such as those cited in this chapter, to justify its conclusions (see *A Study of Coal Prices* [Washington: U.S. Government Printing Office, 1967]).

complete misunderstanding of what is involved. The oil companies, together with electric utilities, existing coal companies, and others, have indeed been accumulating reserves in the western United States with the objective, at least in the next decade or so, of being able to participate in the development of strip-mining in the region. As discussed later, this will largely mean production for sale to electric utilities, and with so many companies potentially involved already, vigorous competition should arise. Moreover, with the potential for additional leasing, even greater competition could emerge once a federal leasing policy is defined. In short, the fears over competition and the need to modify U.S. coal policies radically to account for the potential for monopoly seem, at best, hard to justify.

At least to the extent that *An Energy Policy for Canada* still reflects Canadian attitudes, foreign ownership rather than monopoly has been the primary concern about the structure of the energy industries. The extent of this concern is not clear. Some of the government-owned electric utilities in western Canada have chosen to develop their own coal mines but have decided to seek, or are considering, arrangements with established coal-mining companies, which may not necessarily be Canadian, to manage the mines. Moreover, it can be argued that the number and the size of the Canadian companies — notably those controlled by Canadian Pacific and the Mannix group — becoming involved in coal will lead to considerably less foreign dominance than occurred in oil production.

Given the perspectives of this study, another frequently expressed aspect of the foreign ownership issue — its potential deleterious effect on mineral processing in Canada — seems less likely to be relevant to coal than to other minerals. This study sees only limited prospects for the manufacture of high-quality synthetic fuels from coal — the only kind of processing in which the choice of processing site could be an issue. (However, as noted above, the Alberta government believes otherwise and is acting to reserve coals for synthetic-fuel production.) The great distances that lie between the coal mines and consumer markets suggest that coal cleaning at the mine site will be extensively employed. The reduction in bulk will produce transportation cost savings that will justify the expense of cleaning. Similarly, coke manufacture is conventionally conducted near steel mills because it is most economical to assemble the different kinds of coal used in the coking blend near the point of use. Finally, the use of coal to generate electricity is currently planned only in Canadian plants.

4

Coal Resources and the Economics of Coal Production

For many years Americans have been told that the presence of virtually unlimited supplies of coal throughout much of the United States assured a prosperous, long-term future based on an abundant, cheap source of fuel. Even today, after the recent upheavals in world petroleum markets, it is not uncommon to have casual observers of the energy scene point out that U.S. coal reserves are at least equal to, if not greater than, the energy contained in Middle East oil reserves. Regretfully, our knowledge of the quantity, quality, and economic viability of coal supplies throughout North America remains very unsatisfactory. Given such limited knowledge, it is hard to justify this popular enthusiasm about the great potential role that coal can play in satisfying energy needs of the future. Accordingly, the purpose of this chapter is to take a closer look at estimates of coal resources in the United States and Canada and to shed some light on the complex problems encountered in actually trying to reach any firm conclusions as to the long-term supply prospects in both countries.

U.S. Reserves

Table 7 gives estimates of U.S. coal reserves according to various measurement concepts currently employed.

None of these figures are compiled to provide an appraisal of proved reserves in the usual sense of those known to be economic at current prices. The U.S. Geological Survey (USGS), the source of the most widely quoted data, hardly considers economic factors. Its figures are estimates of physically available supplies, and the principal distinctions made relate to the comparative precision of the estimates. A variety of efforts have been made to identify more accurately the economically most attractive coal resources. The most recent work of this type has been the publication by the U.S. Bureau of Mines (USBM) of data on the demonstrated coal reserve base for the United States. This base includes only the components of the

TABLE 7

Estimates of U.S. Coal Reserves Based on Different Measurement Concepts
(billion tons)

1. U.S. Geological Survey estimate of total identified and hypothetical resources		3,968
2. USGS hypothetical resources		2,237
3. USGS identified resources		1,731
of which bituminous	747	
subbituminous	486	
lignite	478	
anthracite and semi-anthracite	20	
4. U.S. Bureau of Mines estimate of coal resource base		437
of which strippable	136	
underground	300	
5. National Petroleum Council estimate of recoverable reserves		150
of which strippable	45	
underground	105	

Sources: Estimates 1-3: Paul Averitt, *Coal Resources of the United States, January 1, 1974*, U.S. Geological Survey Bulletin 1412 (Washington: U.S. Government Printing Office, 1975), p. 15.
         Estimate 4: U.S. Bureau of Mines, *Reserve Base of U.S. Coal by Sulfur Content*, 2 vols. (Washington: U.S. Government Printing Office, 1975).
         Estimate 5: Coal Task Group of the National Petroleum Council, *U.S. Energy Outlook, Coal Availability* (Washington, 1973), p. 22.

USGS estimates that simultaneously are well-measured and meet various rough criteria of economic viability — relating to seam thickness and depth. However, the economic implication of these rules has never been determined, and good reason exists to suspect that the USBM data overstate the availability of coal at current costs. The Bureau's own earlier efforts to identify strippable reserves used more stringent criteria, such as deleting coal under lands in uses that precluded mining. This produced lower estimates, and even these may be too generous, at least for states east of the Mississippi. (The figures show the availability of ample reserves, but industry sources claim that low-cost reserves have become unavailable.)

Further evidence of the problem is provided by the work of the National Petroleum Council. Its estimates were prepared by a two-stage process in which an initial set of criteria relating to the precision of knowledge and to physical conditions was used to reduce coal resource estimates to about 394 billion tons. Then the USBM data on strippable reserves were used to estimate the strippable proportion of these resources. The application of a second, more stringent set of seam-thickness requirements and the assumption of a 50 percent recovery factor led to the conclusion that only 100 billion tons were economically recoverable by underground mining techniques. Thus these efforts to identify how much coal is available in well-identified seams with reasonably favourable mining conditions produce markedly lower figures than those presented by the USGS. Moreover, considerable doubt exists as to whether the methodology used is sufficiently stringent to eliminate all resources that would be significantly more expensive to utilize than coal presently being exploited. The cutoffs may have been too liberal and may have ignored other important influences on costs.[1]

A particularly graphic illustration of the implications of these revised reserve estimates is provided by the USBM figures on strippable reserves in the western states. These reserves amount to about 27 billion tons. Assuming a BTU content of 17 million BTUs per ton, this would mean that a total of 460 quadrillion BTUs of energy would be available. Any large-scale facility to utilize this energy would probably require at least a thirty-year fuel supply to justify its creation, so that about 15.3 quadrillion BTUs would be available annually. This hardly constitutes sufficient energy to permit realization of the vision of fueling the U.S. economy with cheaply strippable western coal. For example, the United States actually consumed 73 quadrillion BTUs in 1974, and the lowest Project Independence estimate of 1985 consumption is 94 quadrillion BTUs.[2]

This does not necessarily imply that the vision of massive dependence on coal is incorrect; it merely shows that *available low-cost* coal supplies do not suffice to ensure the predicted outcome. Thus it becomes an open question whether this vision is totally invalid, overlooks the rising costs associated with heavy reliance on coal, assumes new low-cost reserves will be discovered to cover the shortfall, or expects technical progress to offset depletion. Even if one is more restrained about the potential role of western strip-mining, these reserves are quite considerable (e.g., probably quite sufficient to provide the fossil fuels needed for an electric-power industry undergoing a shift to nuclear power).

---

[1] For an excellent critique of this issue, see Martin B. Zimmerman, "Long-Run Mineral Supply: The Case of Coal in the United States" (Ph.D. diss., Massachusetts Institute of Technology, 1975), pp. 127-211. The key chapters are available as a report of the MIT Energy Laboratory.

[2] The problem is exacerbated when one assumes that the coal will be converted into liquid or gaseous fuels. Energy will be lost in the conversion process. A synthetic-methane process might be 70 percent efficient, so that about 11 quadrillion BTUs of synthetic methane could be produced; this compares to 1974 consumption of 22 quadrillion BTUs of natural gas. Similarly, conversion efficiency in crude oil synthesis might reach 80 percent, so that any use of coal for the purpose of crude oil synthesis would produce 12 quadrillion BTUs of oil compared to 1974 consumption of 34 quadrillion BTUs of oil. The 15 quadrillion BTUs could cover a substantial portion of the 18.3 quadrillion BTUs used to generate electricity in 1974 but would be grossly inadequate for the 35.6-40.9 quadrillion BTUs that Project Independence considers will be needed in its 1985 scenarios of electric-power generation.

Canadian Reserves

Apparently, less exhaustive work has been done on Canadian than on U.S. coal resources, but the available data suggest that the amount of well-established economic resources is subject to considerable uncertainty. Table 8 presents some of the data on coal reserves found in *An Energy Policy for Canada*. The table compares the nationwide estimates to 1970 figures for the three provinces that possess well over 90 percent of the resources.

TABLE 8

Estimates of Canadian Coal Resources
(billion tons)

	Saskatchewan	Alberta	British Columbia	All Provinces[a]
MacKay (1946):[b]				
Mineable coal:				
Probable	13.1	34.4	11.8	61.4
Possible	11.0	13.4	7.0	36.7
Total	24.1	47.8	18.8	98.1
Recoverable coal:[c]				
Probable	6.6	17.2	5.9	31.1
Possible	5.5	6.7	3.5	18.3
Total	12.1	23.9	9.4	49.4
Latour and Chrismas (1970):[d]				
Measured	0.3	2.2	7.3	9.8
Indicated	7.0	32.1	11.2	50.3
Inferred	4.7	12.9	41.0	58.6
Total	12.0	47.2	59.5	118.7

[a] MacKay's estimates are for the whole of Canada, while the Latour and Chrismas estimates cover the three provinces shown.
[b] Dr. B. K. MacKay of the Geological Survey of Canada prepared these estimates for the Royal Commission on Coal (1946).
[c] Assumes 50 percent recovery rate.
[d] B. A. Latour and L. P. Chrismas, *Preliminary Estimate of Measured Coal Resources Including Reassessment of Indicated and Inferred Resources in Western Canada* (Ottawa: Department of Energy, Mines and Resources, 1970), pp. 11-12. "Measured" reserves are based on detailed evidence, such as information from mine working or closely spaced drill holes. "Indicated" or "probable" resources are estimates based upon more widely spaced signs of coal occurrence. (However, MacKay's data combine the measured and probable resources into a single figure.) "Inferred" are possible resources based upon estimates from broad knowledge of the geology of a region. The mineable recoverable distinction is an effort to estimate how much of the coal in place is economically recoverable.

Source: *An Energy Policy for Canada — Phase I*, Vol. 2, pp. 262-64.

Table 9 presents further details breaking down the coal resource data by subregion and coal quality. A critical point to note is that the more-sought-after bituminous coal suited for metallurgical use (and for existing steam boilers) is found mainly in the less accessible

TABLE 9

**Details of Latour and Chrismas Estimates
of Western Canadian Reserves**
(million short tons)

	Measured	Indicated	Inferred	Total
Low and medium volatile bituminous:				
Alberta:				
Inner foothills —				
Luscar formation	542	7,427	3,535	11,504
Inner foothills —				
Kootenay formation	440	12,194	3,831	16,465
Province total	982	19,620	7,367	27,969
British Columbia	6,943	10,775	40,480	58,198
Total both provinces	7,925	30,395	47,847	86,167
High volatile bituminous:				
Alberta outer foothills	—	6,279	3,044	9,322
British Columbia	46	100	173	319
Total both provinces	46	6,379	3,217	9,641
Alberta subbituminous	1,222	6,197	2,530	9,949
Lignite:				
British Columbia	340	300	300	940
Saskatchewan	292	7,024	4,698	12,014
Total both provinces	632	7,324	4,998	12,954

Source: Latour and Chrismas, *op. cit.*

mountainous regions, while the coal found in flat regions similar to those in the U.S. Northern Great Plains is largely subbituminous or lignite. The mining conditions for higher-quality coals are much more difficult because of both the terrain and the pitching, fragmented nature of the seams. Strip-mining is employed, but costs are much higher than for lower-grade coals. Considerable concern exists over how much expansion in the output of such coal could be obtained without sharp increases in prices and costs. Indications are that an increase in output in the neighbourhood of 10 million tons a year would cause no severe problems, but beyond that level adequate information is lacking. (It may be noted, however, that strains on the resources are considered likely to lead eventually to a shift to underground mining by hydraulic methods.)

It can be seen that the two surveys present similar estimates for Alberta, but the 1970 figures are markedly higher for British Columbia and lower for Saskatchewan than the 1946 estimates. Moreover, only a small fraction of these reserves is well-measured, and a sizable portion is inferred.[3] Efforts are under way, however, to de-

---

[3] Note that MacKay's concept of probable reserves is roughly akin to Latour and Chrismas's concepts of measured and indicated reserves.

lineate the economically recoverable resources of coal in western Canada, and preliminary figures indicate 300 million tons are available in Saskatchewan and 1.5 billion in Alberta.[4]

Subsequent work by the Alberta government has indicated that coal resources in the province may amount to as much as 140 billion tons, but this figure can be considered as highly optimistic. Only 5 billion tons of strip-mineable reserves have been proved,[5] and the expectation for the plains region, where 4.3 billion tons of proved strippable reserves exist, is that only 1.3 billion more tons of such reserves are really likely to be found.[6] As a consequence, this has inspired some fear about the adequacy of strippable reserves within the province and has prompted provincial authorities to consider conservation measures.

Predicting Future Supply

Moving from reserve estimates to supply projections is a nearly impossible task. At least three barriers that limit our ability to predict supply can be identified.

First, in a simple world of unchanging input prices and technology, supply could be predicted simply through detailed knowledge of the physical properties of coal seams. In practice, we lack adequate conceptual studies that identify the critical physical factors and their impact on cost. Thus we have no way of knowing whether the available data on the physical properties of coal resources are adequate for cost analysis, and we have good reason to suspect the data are unsatisfactory.[7]

Second, technology and input prices, especially wages, are not stable over time, and forecasts must take these shifts into account. The forecasting procedures are complicated because there are very serious problems in sorting out basic underlying trends from transitional or temporary adjustments. For example, most observers would agree that the retreat of spot prices from the peak levels reached in

[4] Department of Energy, Mines and Resources, *An Energy Policy for Canada — Phase 1*, Vol. 1 (Ottawa: Information Canada, 1973), p. 84.
[5] Alberta Energy Resources Conservation Board, *Review of the Alberta Coal Industry*, 1973 (Calgary, 1974), pp. 3-5 to 3-7.
[6] Alberta Energy Resources Conservation Board, *The Adequacy of Alberta's Reserves of Surface Mineable Subbituminous Coal to Meet Market Requirements* (Calgary, 1974) p. 6.
[7] See Zimmerman (*op. cit.*, pp. 125-57) for an impressive demonstration of this argument. He notes that most underground-mine-costing models consider only the effect of seam thickness on costs. By elaborate statistical analysis, he shows that such studies grossly understate both the impact of seam thickness and the influence of other factors on costs. A review of existing cost studies published through early 1975 can be found in Richard L. Gordon, *Economic Analysis of Coal Supply — An Assessment of Existing Studies* (Palo Alto: Electric Power Research Institute, 1975) (subsequent references shorten the title to *Economic Analysis*). An identically titled sequel appeared in 1976 and contains a review of Zimmerman.

1974 will continue as capacity becomes better adjusted to the new demand conditions. On the other hand, given such problems as the conflict between pressures to secure compliance with sulfur-emission regulations and efforts to restrain mining of western coal, capacity will be much slower in adjusting to longer-run demand changes, and this will mean that the price slide will be much more moderate.

Similar issues exist about the behaviour of labour costs. The need to attract new workers into the industry has already caused sharp rises in real wages. Costs have also increased as underground output per man-day declined following the implementation of the Coal Mine Health and Safety Act. Finally, the industry has suffered from frequent wildcat strikes caused by dissension among the United Mine Workers. Considerable debate can be raised about whether labour unrest and rising wages are temporary problems or an inevitable aspect of the dirty, dangerous occupation of underground coal mining.

Third, it should be evident from the discussion in Chapter 3 that a variety of public policies currently under review could change in ways that would have a measurable impact on the future supply situation in the United States. Two key questions concern the extent to which the impact of the Health and Safety Act will abate as the industry becomes familiar with the rules and to what degree the regulatory process creates a climate inimical to productivity recovery and advance.

Regional Considerations

No analysis of the outlook for coal in either Canada or the United States would be complete without some reference to the heterogeneous nature of the industry. This heterogeneity exists on two levels. First, as I have noted repeatedly, the physical properties of coal differ according to whether a particular deposit is best suited for metallurgical or steam coal purposes; in addition, the degree of sulfur content must be considered for environmental reasons. Second, the long-range supply potential ultimately hinges on mining conditions, which vary considerably throughout individual producing regions in both countries. What follows is a brief overview of the regional characteristics of coal and their implications for future supplies.

Looking at the United States first, there are two major regions that have traditionally supplied coal for domestic and export markets — Appalachia and the eastern interior or midwestern region. The former stretches from Pennsylvania to Alabama, and the latter encompasses Illinois, Indiana, and western Kentucky. As we shall see later on, considerable interest has developed recently in exploiting coal regions west of the Mississippi — notably in Montana, Wyoming, and North Dakota.

As far as Appalachia is concerned, the two most important considerations are the availability of metallurgical coal (i.e., coal suitable for manufacturing coke for the production of pig iron) and the relatively greater difficulty that exists in mining coal in the East. Appalachia (or, more precisely, a portion of Appalachia in Pennsylvania, West Virginia, and Kentucky) has the most ample supplies of coking coal in the United States, but mining conditions are generally less favourable than in other parts of the country, especially in the case of strip-mining. Given these less favourable conditions and the fact that the mining of coking coal, in general, is more difficult than of other types of coal, the exploitation of this vast supply of eastern coal may become increasingly more expensive as time goes on.

Costs could also surge in the Midwest in the future. Since the end of World War II, strip-mining has become the dominant mining method in the Midwest, but it now appears that any substantial expansion of output in the region will require a considerable shift towards more expensive underground mining procedures. The only remaining significant region suitable for low-cost strip-mining is west of the Mississippi River. However, as was mentioned earlier, there are a number of serious policy issues affecting western lands that have to be resolved before any legitimate cost assessment can be made.

Given the environmental concerns discussed in Chapter 3, the sulfur content of coal is also a key factor of future supply conditions. Most coal mined east of the Mississippi is too high in sulfur content to meet environmental restrictions, and considerable controversy exists about the potential ability to produce environmentally acceptable coal in Appalachia. In contrast, much western coal is low in sulfur content. Until the middle 1970s, the low heat content of the fuel and the long distance between the coal fields and major markets created considerable doubts about its immediate widespread use.

Similarly, qualitative differences exist among coal-producing regions in Canada. Most observers consider the resources in Nova Scotia too expensive to be a promising large-scale energy source; accordingly, the greatest interest lies in the coal deposits of western provinces. Subbituminous coal and lignite in Alberta and Saskatchewan can be mined at low cost, are low in sulfur content, and might be a source of energy for industry in eastern Canada if transportation costs could be reduced substantially. Both British Columbia and Alberta produce coal of metallurgical quality, but high mining and transportation costs continue to make it unattractive for eastern consumers. At present, Canada finds it more profitable to export this valuable coal and rely on coal from Appalachia to meet domestic coking coal needs. For reasons reviewed in Chapter 5, however, higher-quality Alberta coal is a likely candidate to replace some of the U.S. coal currently used for electric-power generation in Ontario.

To sum up, the outlook for coal costs is complicated by the qualitative differences among the various producing regions, and a careful weighing of these considerations is needed in order to arrive at an overall appraisal of the long-term supply outlook in the industry.

Outlook for Coal Costs

With these warnings in mind, we can attempt to trace roughly the general coal supply situation in the United States and Canada. Before doing so, a word of caution is needed. The cost figures given in this chapter cannot, by themselves, be employed to evaluate the competitive position of coal, since no simple, direct comparison with the prices of other fuels is valid. The competitive position of coal in a market requires comparison of the total costs — i.e., all operating expenses and the required rate of return on investment — of alternative energy sources. In Chapter 5 an attempt is made to translate these coal price estimates into total cost analyses for comparison with the cost of generating electricity with nuclear energy.

The weight of available evidence suggests that, even for coal relatively high in sulfur content and suitable only for non-metallurgical use, output at or well above 1975 levels can be secured east of the Mississippi only if both underground mines and strip-mines are operated. The continued existence of underground mines and the tendency of even leading companies previously stressing strip-mining to open underground mines suggest that, to expand output substantially, it is cheaper to exploit available underground resources than available strip resources. In this regard, widely published figures, such as those produced by the U.S. Bureau of Mines, about the much lower costs of hypothetical large strip-mines are essentially irrelevant, since the blocks of coal needed to develop such mines are apparently no longer available on a wide scale.

The situation is even worse for costing mines producing low-sulfur, metallurgical-grade coal. Not only are strippable reserves very scarce, but the conditions for underground mining appear more unfavourable. In contrast, as noted, as long as relatively modest amounts of coal are involved, strippable resources in states in the Northern Great Plains appear capable of meeting the requirements without substantial increases in costs. A similar proposition seems to apply to the subbituminous and lignite steam coal of Alberta and Saskatchewan, but the supply potential of metallurgical coal in British Columbia and Alberta is less clear. Too few data exist on potential mining conditions to provide even rough cost estimates.

As a starting point, the data reported in the appendix to this chapter suggest that, in terms of 1975 dollars, the long-run cost, f.o.b. mine, is 55-90 cents per million BTUs for eastern steam coal and 15-30 cents per million BTUs for coal mined in the U.S. Northern Great Plains regions and the more accessible Canadian strip-mineable coal found in Alberta and British Columbia.

There is, however, a considerable divergence of opinion among various observers of the industry concerning estimates of the future course of costs. Prospective developments depend critically upon the net impact of a host of major factors principally:

- the pressure for higher real wages for miners as a means of inducing a whole new generation of young workers to take up coal mining as a long-term occupation;
- the behaviour of productivity (output per man-day) in an industry where productivity levels have actually declined significantly in recent years as a result of major changes in health and safety laws;
- other additional cost increases originating in new mining regulations.

In particular, it is too soon to say to what extent future productivity gains can effectively offset the rising real costs of labour; this is especially true in the case of underground mining, where labour costs are a significantly greater proportion of total operating costs than they are in strip-mining.

With these considerations in mind, the appendix to this chapter develops a range of estimates for future U.S. coal prices. Briefly, in the case of eastern steam coal, the optimistic assumption is that cost (rounded to the nearest $0.05) remains at 55 cents per million BTUs in 1975 dollars through to 1980; the pessimistic assumptions call for a rise (in 1975 dollars) from 90 cents in 1975 to $1.10 in 1980, $1.30 in 1985, and $1.65 in 1990. Metallurgical coal costs in Appalachia are estimated at twice steam coal costs. U.S. and Canadian western strip-mines for subbituminous and lignite are assumed able to meet demands over the period covered here at costs similar to those prevailing in 1975.

Delivered prices are difficult to characterize because so many origin-destination combinations must be considered. Historically, the dominant mode of transportation has been by rail, and even if we confine our attention to rail, numerous complications can arise. For example, the railroads west of the Mississippi are largely lower-cost and in a stronger financial position than those in the East. Moreover, because of either administrative difficulties or a desire to limit loss of movement of local coal, rates for continuation of rail trips eastward from the terminals of western roads are often unattractive.[8]

These problems, and the lower costs of water transportation, have inspired dual-mode movements of western coal. Detroit Edison

---

[8] This argument is developed at length by Zimmerman, *op. cit.*

has arranged for rail shipment of coal to Lake Superior for trans-shipment by lake vessel; a similar concept is being developed for construction of a transfer point from rail to vessel at Thunder Bay, Ontario. Also, American Electric Power is arranging transfer from trains to river barges at Metropolis and East St. Louis, Illinois. Ontario Hydro's receipts of U.S. coal have long involved rail-vessel combinations.

Substantial amounts of coal can move from eastern states to major markets entirely by barge. Other alternatives are to build power plants near the coal mines and ship electricity or to pipeline the coal. A flurry of proposals for building plants near coal fields to serve distant markets emerged in the late sixties, but the movement seems largely to have been aborted subsequently (although many of the plants previously conceived remain uncompleted). Public policy problems seem to have been a major cause of the change in attitude west of the Mississippi. Stringent air-pollution regulations, water-rights problems, and the need to prepare Environmental Impact Statements for power lines have all lessened the attractiveness of plants near mines. In 1973 the Secretary of the Interior prohibited construction of the last and largest of a series of coal-fired plants in the Southwest.[9] The lessened interest of the eastern electric-power industry seems to be largely the result of pessimism over coal use in general.

Coal has been successfully pipelined as a slurry of water and fine particles, and some work has been conducted on pneumatic pipelining. The principal barrier to pipelining is that such pipelines would have to cross rail lines, and the legal power to prevent obstruction by the railroads has not been granted. Again, problems concerning water rights and Environmental Impact Statements would be involved.

Thus the pattern and the cost of coal transportation in the United States are subject to particularly great uncertainty. The available literature suggests that, by 1980, U.S. coal transportation costs, in 1975 dollars, are likely to be no less than a penny per ton-mile, and under unfavourable circumstances might easily be double this amount.[10]

---

[9] The utilities involved instituted efforts to reverse the decision, and in the spring of 1976 the Interior Department had modified its position sufficiently to have issued a Final Environmental Impact Statement on the project, called Kaparowits — a preliminary step towards granting approval. Although the Secretary of the Interior was widely expected to grant approval, the utilities involved canceled the project.

[10] The conclusions on coal transportation costs are a rough synthesis of a wide variety of material including studies reported in Gordon, *Economic Analysis, op. cit.*; Zimmerman's thesis, pp. 37-72; P. H. Mutschler, R. J. Evans, and G. M. Larwood, *Comparative Transportation Costs of Supplying Low-Sulfur Fuels to Midwestern and Eastern Domestic Energy Markets*, U.S. Bureau of Mines Information Circular 8614 (Washington: U.S. Government Printing Office, 1973); and U.S. Federal Energy Administration, *Project Independence Blueprint Final Task Force Report*,

(Cont'd on page 43)

As we shall see in the next chapter, the prospects for using western Canadian coal in Ontario hinge on developing adequate low-cost methods for shipping coal from western Canada. However, proposals have been made to solve this problem by developing a combined rail-water transportation system in which unit trains would move the coal to Thunder Bay, Ontario, where a transfer facility would be constructed to facilitate loading for Lake shipment to southern Ontario.

Because this facility might be used for a wide variety of coal, it is preferable that the cost estimates be stated on a per-ton basis to provide means for applying the figures to any grade of coal we wish to consider. The cost could amount to $20-23 per ton. Rail transportation to Thunder Bay, using cars and power supplied by the consumer, would cost $13 per ton. The implicit cost of cars and power to the buyer amounts to about $3 per ton if a private firm borrowed; a government entity might finance cars and power for about $2 per ton. A further $3-per-ton cost would be incurred at Thunder Bay for the expenses of handling and storage over the period during which the Great Lakes are frozen. Lake shipping costs would add another $2-4 per ton to costs. In any case, the facilities have yet to be built, and the substantial investments involved have made some potential Canadian consumers of the coal skeptical about the wisdom of a switch to Canadian coal.

(Cont'd from page 42)

Analysis of Requirements and Constraints on the Transport of Energy Materials, Vol. 1, and *Inputs to the Project Independence Evaluation System Integration Model for the Transport of Energy Materials*, Vol. 2 (Washington: U.S. Government Printing Office, 1974).

Appendix to Chapter 4

Prospective Coal-Mining Costs

For the reasons outlined in the main text of this chapter, a satisfactory basis for projecting coal prices does not exist. For present purposes, therefore, a range of possible future prices has been constructed by crudely combining 1975 reports of prices on long-term coal purchase contracts, the cost data in the coal volume of the Project Independence Blueprint (PIB), and the author's earlier projections of coal cost trends.[1]

A new publication, *Coal Week*, reports prices on long-term contracts, and its data indicate that prices for high-sulfur midwestern coal on long-term contracts range from $15 to $22 per ton. The head of the Tennessee Valley Authority argues that these prices are still inflated by the aftermath of the sharp price rises of 1974 and that a more appropriate price would be around $12 per ton. As to what seems to be the most optimistic reasonable assumption, it may be assumed that ultimately a $12 price can be reached and maintained indefinitely. (Project Independence assumes no increase in coal-mining costs over time. It is not clear whether this simply reflected lack of time to develop projections or a true belief that costs could be kept stable.) Project Independence set northern Appalachian costs 29 percent above those in the Midwest; applying this factor to the $12 price implies a price of $15.50. This ratio may exaggerate the difference in steam coal costs, since the Appalachian average is raised by the inclusion of metallurgical coal, which is more expensive to extract. As a crude adjustment for the bias, it can arbitrarily be assumed that steam coal costs in Appalachia are only 15 percent above those in the Midwest (i.e., half the differential). This leads to a price of $14 a ton.

A pessimistic forecast can be developed by assuming that the midwest price is currently $19 per ton and that in Appalachia, $22. In a previous study, I argued that real wages in underground coal mining would rise from 6 to 12 percent per year.[2] I will use the

---

[1] R. L. Gordon, *U.S. Coal and the Electric Power Industry* (Baltimore: Johns Hopkins University Press for Resources for the Future, 1975).

[2] *Ibid.*, p. 115.

higher estimate, the assumption of a 4-percent-per-year increase in output per man-day (OMD), and the assumption that 1975 labour costs constitute about 40 percent of the required selling price. The productivity forecast was selected as being slightly more optimistic than the 2.7 percent annual increase estimated by Harry Perry, a long-time observer of the coal industry.[3] The PIB mine studies indicate that labour costs range from 36 to 51 percent of the required selling price of different sizes and types of model mines. Two assumptions are behind the choice of 40 percent as the ratio. First, it was assumed that marginal mines of the future were likely to be characterized by a lower ratio of labour cost to selling price because of higher investment in production facilities. Second, it was assumed that the 1974 UMW contract raised the ratio of labour cost to price for each type of mine, so that higher ratios than used by PIB are appropriate.

Table 10 converts these assumptions into estimates of future f.o.b. mine prices. (I have chosen not to round during the interim calculations because this makes the derivation easier to follow, even though it imparts a spurious precision to the figures.) The end results should be interpreted as an optimistic forecast of a price of about $0.55 per million BTUs throughout the period and a pessimistic forecast of prices of $0.90 in 1975, $1.10 in 1980, $1.30 in 1985, and $1.65 in 1990. Metallurgical-grade coal appears to sell for at least double the cost of steam coal — say $40 a ton. Taking account of the higher BTU content involved, a tentative forecast would be to double the price-per-million-BTUs figures used for Appalachian steam coal.

At the time of writing, the U.S. Federal Energy Administration had issued revised energy forecasts in its *National Energy Outlook* report. Assuming stable constant-dollar cost estimates, the report reworked coal supply estimates. According to the computer printouts, the model calculated that the 1985 equilibrium price for f.o.b. mined coal is in the range of 55 to 60 cents per million BTUs for eastern high-sulfur steam coal and 25 cents per million BTUs for Northern Great Plains subbituminous coal.[4]

Price forecasts for western strip-mined coal range from $2.50 to $5.00 a ton for 16.5 million BTUs per ton of coal — or 15 to 30 cents per million BTUs. Comparable prices apparently will prevail for strip-mined steam coal in the plains of Saskatchewan and Alberta.

Evidence is less clear about Canadian coking coals, but Canadian sources suggest that prices of about $40 per ton f.o.b. mine and $50 per ton f.o.b. the West Coast prevail.

---

[3] See R. L. Gordon, *Economic Analysis of Coal Supply — An Assessment of Existing Studies* (Palo Alto: Electric Power Research Institute, 1975), pp. 111-12.
[4] U.S. Federal Energy Administration, *National Energy Outlook* (Washington: U.S. Government Printing Office, 1976), p. 206.

TABLE 10

Computation of Forecasts of Underground-Coal-Mining Costs, Eastern United States, 1975-90

Basic assumptions for pessimistic case

	Appalachia	Midwest
1. Initial (1975) price ($/ton)	22.00	19.00
2. Labour cost as percentage of 1975 price	40.00	40.00
3. 1975 labour cost ($/ton) (1 times 2)	8.80	7.60
4. 1975 non-labour costs (1 minus 3)	13.20	11.40
5. Average annual percentage increase in labour costs per man-day	12.0	12.0
6. Average annual increase in output per man-day	4.0	4.0
7. Average annual percentage increase in labour cost per ton ([1.12/1.04] - 1.0)	7.7	7.7
8. Percentage increase in labour costs per five-year period ($1.077^5 - 1$)	44.9	44.9

Unrounded estimates of future costs ($/ton except as noted)

A. *Optimistic Case*

	Appalachia				Midwest			
	Non-Labour Costs	Labour Costs	Total Costs	Total Costs: Dollars/ Million BTUs	Non-Labour Costs	Labour Costs	Total Costs	Total Costs: Dollars/ Million BTUs
1975-90	n.a.	n.a.	14.00	0.58	n.a.	n.a.	12.00	0.57

B. *Pessimistic Case*

1975	13.20	8.80	22.00	0.92	11.40	7.60	19.00	0.90
1980	13.20	12.75	25.95	1.08	11.40	11.01	22.41	1.07
1985	13.20	18.46	31.66	1.32	11.40	15.95	27.35	1.30
1990	13.20	26.75	39.95	1.66	11.40	23.10	34.50	1.64

n.a. = not applicable.
Source: See text.

5

Market Prospects for Coal

In the United States, at least, discussions of coal stress that it is "our most abundant fuel." This slogan presumably should be taken to imply that coal will once again assume a dominant role in U.S. energy markets. In the previous chapter it was suggested that the existence of large amounts of coal does not guarantee that all this coal will be cheap to produce. In this chapter, the whole vision of increased reliance on coal is evaluated by considering the potential forces influencing the market for coal.

Basically, those envisioning a major swing towards coal expect that there will be a further extension of coal in its current markets as well as the development of coal as a substitute source for crude oil and natural gas. This chapter develops three basic propositions about this argument. First, it shows that there are actually enormous long-term problems in maintaining the role of coal in existing markets. Second, the development of synthetic fuels from coal will require many years of effort, and at this early date success is by no means assured. Third, this vision of the abundance of coal may be even less applicable to Canada than to the United States. In short, abundance is not equivalent to an easy solution to energy problems.

To evaluate the prospects for coal, it is essential to consider explicitly the nature of the myriad activities aggregated under the umbrella of energy consumption. These various uses of energy differ markedly in their inherent flexibility in fuel choice. Moreover, once an individual consumer selects an option, his flexibility from an economic point of view is greatly reduced because conversion to another fuel may require expensive investments that act as a deterrent in making a switch.

Fuel-Choice Restrictions

Final users of fuels can be crudely differentiated according to three basic degrees of flexibility (at least when only the technology of the fuel used is considered):

- those who can use any form of fossil fuel or electricity;
- those who have unlimited ability to employ fossil fuels but cannot use electricity; and
- those who must use specific fuels.

47

Examples of uses in the first and last categories should be familiar to everyone. Clearly, heating of homes, offices, and other structures can be provided by any fossil fuel or electricity, whereas most transportation systems must use specialized fuels (e.g., gasoline and diesel oil are the only currently practical alternatives for road transportation).

The second category primarily includes producers of electricity itself and manufacturers of chemical feedstocks based on fossil fuels. Anyone who is able to use all fossil fuels is probably essentially consuming heat and chooses the cheapest heat source. If the costs are favourable, electricity could also be selected.

After the consumer chooses a particular fuel, the loss of flexibility is measured in terms of the cost of conversion. For example, a boiler designed to burn coal can easily convert to natural gas; all that is necessary is to install the pipes for the gas and make other minor modifications. However, a boiler designed for gas may have tubes too small to permit coal use. (Indeed, boilers designed for one type of coal may not be able to burn other types easily.) To convert from, say, oil to electric heating requires a completely new heating system.

Air-pollution regulations and the technologies available to permit compliance impose further restrictions on fuel choice. Some control technologies are unlikely to be practical except for large-scale energy users. The present principal pollution problem with stationary uses of fossil fuel concerns sulfur oxides.[1] Automotive pollution can be ignored here because it has no significant impact on the prospects for coal. The logical possibilities for sulfur-oxide-pollution control are to use a naturally low-sulfur fuel, to reduce the sulfur content of high-sulfur fuels, or to burn high-sulfur fuels and employ devices known as stack gas scrubbers to capture and prevent the emission of the sulfur oxides.[2] Stack gas scrubbers have proven to be expensive, difficult-to-operate devices that usually produce sludges of

[1] Actually, sulfur oxides are only one of three pollutants emitted in significant amounts in stationary combustion processes. However, control requirements for the second — particulates, the solid material emitted — can generally be met by use of proven technologies. Control requirements for the third, nitrogen oxides, have not yet been made stringent enough to create control problems. It is conceivable, of course, that standards on both these other pollutants might be tightened to a degree that would create severe control problems. For example, some observers express concern that the very small particulates not captured by existing control devices are far more dangerous than the particle emissions actually controlled and suggest stringent controls in the area. Similarly, significant difficulties have arisen in controlling nitrogen oxide emissions from coal-burning facilities.

[2] Another approach is to build very tall smoke stacks to spread emissions over a wide area and to shut down or shift to low-sulfur fuel when weather conditions make the emission particularly dangerous. This strategy is vigorously advocated by some leading electric utilities and widely attacked by environmentalists. The key point at issue is whether this is an adequate degree of control. A secondary argument is whether the need to adopt emergency measures can be anticipated sufficiently rapidly to permit effective response.

sulfur and limestone used to capture the sulfur. Thus only large-scale fuel users such as electric utilities are likely to find scrubber use economically feasible.

The variety of pretreatment possibilities is considerable. In the case of coal, these range from simple physical cleaning of the coal to removal of the sulfur during the creation of a high-grade fuel such as a synthetic methane or crude oil. An intermediate step would be to undertake the cleanup during a simpler and, therefore, cheaper chemical transformation, such as the manufacture of a low-quality gas. Because such low-grade fuels would be expensive to transport, they would be used only by large-scale consumers who could install the fuel-processing plants near where the fuel would be used. However, existing technologies for extracting simple synthetic fuels from coal apparently are even more expensive than stack gas scrubbers. Such a conclusion was reached by the Tennessee Valley Authority after conducting a review of scrubber economics for the Environmental Protection Agency and a review of synthetic-fuel economics for the Electric Power Research Institute.[3] (Desulfurization of natural gas is a simpler process that was routinely employed to prevent pipeline corrosion long before concern over sulfur air pollution arose. Oil desulfurization can be more difficult, depending on the crude oil and the degree of desulfurization desired. Even so, the costs are modest compared to those involved in the cleanup of coal.)[4]

Sulfur oxide pollution from oil and gas has not been a serious concern because supplies of naturally low-sulfur oil and gas have been readily available and pretreatment has been only a modest problem. However, the availability of low-sulfur coal has been a highly controversial issue, at least in the United States. It is widely agreed that substantial low-sulfur coal reserves exist west of the Mississippi. The main long-term concerns about this coal have been the high cost of transporting it to major markets and the social and environmental impacts on the West of massive mining developments.[5] Possible bottlenecks in the supply of mining equipment and transportation facilities may be a short-term problem. A bitter

---

[3] G. G. McGlamery et al., Detailed Cost Estimates for Advanced Effluent Desulfurization Processes, Environmental Protection Technology Series EPA 600/2-75-006 (Washington: U.S. Government Printing Office, 1975); and D. A. Waitzman et al., Evaluation of Fixed-Bed, Low BTU Coal Gasification Systems for Retrofitting Power Plants (Palo Alto: Electric Power Research Institute, 1975).

[4] R. L. Gordon, U.S. Coal and the Electric Power Industry (Baltimore: Johns Hopkins University Press for Resources for the Future, 1975), pp. 130 and 172-78.

[5] Rieber has noted the further problem that the coal has a relatively low BTU content, and as I noted above, the lower the BTU content, the lower the percentage weight sulfur content that meets the EPA limits on sulfur emissions per million BTUs. The data on the percentage weight sulfur content of western coals are presented in a fashion that makes it difficult to deduce how much coal actually meets EPA standards (see Michael Rieber, Low Sulfur Coal: A Revision of Reserve and Supply Estimates [Urbana: Center for Advanced Computation, University of Illinois, 1973]).

argument has arisen over the extent to which one can secure low-sulfur coal in Appalachia economically. Reserve data using U.S. Geological Survey concepts indicate the availability of vast amounts of low-sulfur coal in southern West Virginia and eastern Kentucky. However, the magnitude of these estimates was substantially reduced by adoption of the U.S. Bureau of Mines (USBM) reserve-base concept, and many observers suggest that even the USBM approach gives inadequate recognition to the high costs associated with massive development of such reserves.[6]

The choice of fuel is further complicated by lead-time constraints. Merely to construct a complex industrial facility using established technology can be quite time-consuming. Under ideal conditions, a conventional steam turbine, fossil-fuel-fired electric plant takes five years to build. The lead time for a nuclear plant may be ten years (although much, if not all, of the extra time may be due to regulatory barriers). Similar lead-time constraints exist on the development of coal mines and facilities to transport the coal to market. Clearly, when the technology has not been fully perfected, as is true with stack gas scrubbing and coal-synthesis processes, further delays are involved.[7] Even when these technologies are perfected, considerable time will be required to develop the production and construction capabilities to install them on the scale required to attain current air-pollution objectives. Similar problems may arise in training operating manpower. Thus it may prove socially undesirable to seek *rapid* changes in U.S. energy consumption practices. The *extra* costs of faster attainment of environmental goals may exceed the benefits.

Unfortunately, all these preliminaries lead only to the conclusion that it is nearly impossible to predict the level and form of future coal use in the United States and Canada, or the source of this coal. A few obvious points can be made, however. The lead times in the synthetic-fuel realm are such that, whatever the long-run economic prospects, only modest amounts of coal synthesis are

---

[6] Gordon (*U.S. Coal, op. cit.,* p. 110) reached this conclusion on the basis of discussion with coal and electric-utility sources; Martin B. Zimmerman ("Long-Run Mineral Supply: The Case of Coal in the United States" [Ph.D. diss., Massachusetts Institute of Technology, 1975], pp. 159-84) provides a statistical demonstration of the scarcity of such reserves. Press reports have periodically presented contrary views by environmentalists, the United Mine Workers, and, most recently, the West Virginia legislature.

[7] The statement in the text deliberately sidesteps the controversies about how close to perfection the various processes are. The latest data available suggest that, while a few stack-gas-scrubbing installations have attained reliability, others still have difficulties to overcome. EPA has so often prematurely proclaimed scrubber availability that caution is needed, but it does seem that, at long last, reliable scrubbers appear likely to become available shortly. Several workable processes for low-BTU gases do exist, but most observers feel that better, cheaper processes must be developed before the widespread manufacture of low-BTU gas from coal will become feasible.

likely to occur until well into the 1980s. Over this same time horizon, many present users of oil and natural gas may find it prohibitively expensive to shift to direct coal burning or electrification.[8] Some observers believe that electrification will be a major development but that nuclear power will be the primary source of electricity. However, the long lead times in nuclear plants are such that a nuclear takeover would also take many years to develop.[9]

Progress towards reliance on nuclear power in the United States has indeed been retarded by a rash of delays and cancellations caused by financial difficulties arising in the fall of 1974. In contrast, Canada's plans for a shift to nuclear power have proceeded much more rapidly, to the point that Ontario Hydro projects that by 1983 about a quarter of its capacity, and presumably even more of its output, will be from nuclear plants.[10]

In short, difficult transitional problems are involved in the development of new and different forms of energy in the United States and, perhaps to a lesser degree, Canada. It may be impossible, or at least inordinately expensive, to attain ambitious goals for improving the environment and reducing energy imports rapidly and simultaneously. (Indeed, even one of these goals would probably be difficult to attain quickly even if the other were totally abandoned.) Data to measure the costs of possible energy developments during this interim period are largely non-existent. The most that can be said is that many qualitative indicators exist that suggest that serious problems would be produced by policies that press for too rapid attainment of the many ambitious energy objectives proposed in recent years. Thus serious reconsideration should be made of the timetables and, for that matter, of some of the more extreme

---

[8] This is graphically illustrated by the resistance that has arisen over efforts of the U.S. Federal Energy Administration (FEA) in 1975 to force a number of electric-power plants to shift back to coal use. Some of these plants removed the facilities needed to receive, store, and handle coal and dedicated the land to other uses. Others are so old and near retirement that reconversion to coal would be extremely expensive on a per-kilowatt-hour basis, since the costs must be spread over a low quantity of generation. All are concerned about securing low-sulfur coal or emission-control equipment that will permit conversion without violation of sulfur-emission regulations.

[9] Nuclear power, of course, is no environmental panacea; one trades radiation problems for air pollution. In particular, there are serious questions about radiation releases through accidents at nuclear power plants and fuel-processing facilities or through failures in the systems needed to store radioactive wastes that remain dangerous for thousands of years. Others fear diversion of nuclear material to terrorist groups. The present study assumes that the problems with nuclear power and coal are both technically solvable. This is to be considered less a firm judgment about the actual developments than a desire to avoid resolving the difficult issue of fuel choice by an *ex cathedra* environmental evaluation that I am not competent to make.

[10] See Province of Ontario, *Prospectus*, June 11, 1975, p. 32. Since nuclear plants have low running costs, they are likely to be more heavily utilized and thus to contribute more than 25 percent of output.

environmental proposals based on very high values assigned implicitly to aesthetic benefits.[11]

Electricity Generation

Once we get past the transition period, many different scenarios
can be envisioned. At least two basic cases can be traced out analy-
tically. In one case, all but those fuel users incapable of doing so
would shift to electricity. In the other case, electrification would
continue to increase its penetration of the energy market, but large
portions of the economy would continue direct use of fossil fuels. Of
course, many variant cases, combining elements of both basic scenarios, may deserve examination. Industrial users of fossil fuels and
generated steam might begin to concentrate near each other, so that
central steam systems using direct burning of coal, manufacture and
use of low-grade synthetic fuels, or even nuclear boilers might be
installed. Alternatively, these industrial users might remain dis-
persed and continue oil and gas use or find economical ways to use
coal. Similarly, one can imagine many different distributions of oil
and gas supplies among such sources as conventional crude oil and
natural gas, tar sands, oil shales, and coal.

Even if this study were more comprehensive, it could not hope
to resolve these issues. No one possesses the data required for such
an evaluation. Instead, the study concentrates on prospective
developments in electric-power generation and coal for pig iron
manufacture. Here a fortunate combination of circumstances prevails. The two sectors, as the predominant current users of coal, are
the ones in which the most immediate developments affecting coal
will arise. In particular, the key issue in Canadian-U.S. coal
relationships is the supply of fuel to the electric-power and steel
industries of Ontario. Because coal use is so well-established in
these sectors, considerable data are available on the factors affecting
fuel choice. I am thus in the fortunate position that the most pressing issues are the ones I can best analyze.[12]

Moreover, an appraisal of the electric-power case will not only
help to evaluate the ability of coal to retain its present major market but will also provide some basis for comparing the economics of
different approaches to the longer-term problem of large-scale heat
generation.[13]

---

[11] The final report of the Energy Policy Project of the Ford Foundation, *A Time to
Choose* (Cambridge, Mass.: Ballinger Publishing Company, 1974), in its zero-
growth scenario, for example, seems to object to such energy developments as
offshore oil and gas drilling purely on such aesthetic grounds and overlooks that
such offshore drilling is one of the least-polluting energy alternatives available.

[12] This does not mean that no uncertainties exist, but only that they seem much
smaller than those involved with other sectors of the energy economy.

[13] The equally critical issues of the comparative economics of heat generation in
smaller facilities and how demands for high-quality fuels will be met can be
treated only briefly because of the lack of adequate data.

Outlook for Electric-Power Generation in the United States

Looking at the United States first, the analysis of U.S. electric-power generation involves two stages. First, I attempt an appraisal of the optimal fuel choice for new or planned U.S. coal-fired plants using the standard steam turbine technology now dominantly employed in electric-power generation from fossil fuel and nuclear power.[14] To simplify the analysis, I assume that sulfur-emission standards comparable to the EPA specific-source rule will ultimately apply to all plants.[15] Then I look at the longer run, where nuclear power and alternative generating techniques are relevant and viable options. Many such options have been proposed, but here the "combined-cycle" alternative is used as the quintessence of such new technologies.

Two considerations justify choice of the combined-cycle method. First, the combined cycle itself is an established technology already in use. A combined cycle involves first using a gas turbine (a stationary adaptation of a jet engine) to rotate a generator. Since the exit temperature of the gas from the gas turbine is hot enough to produce steam, a heat-recovery boiler can be added to the gas turbine to capture the waste heat, produce steam, and use the steam to rotate another generator. Second, cost data are available on the combined cycle and on the low-BTU gas from coal it might use. This should by no means be taken as a forecast that the combined cycle will be the best alternative method of generating electricity from coal to emerge (or that any such method will prove economic). Serious questions exist about attaining sufficiently inexpensive processes for low-BTU gas. (On the other hand, most alternatives also require use of coal in a transformed form and require considerably more technical development than the combined cycle.)

Using cost data for fossil fuel, nuclear power, and low-BTU gas found in the Project Independence Blueprint estimate, three types of coal-burning plants are costed: (1) a steam turbine burning bituminous coal high enough in sulfur content to require stack gas scrubbers; (2) a steam turbine using lignite low enough in sulfur content not to require scrubbers; and (3) a combined cycle using low-BTU gas from coal. Costs and performance characteristics for the steam turbines are estimated for 1980, 1985, and 1990 completion, but only 1985 and 1990 figures are given for the combined cycle using coal gas (because the low-BTU gas processes will not be available in 1980).

---

[14] The system simply involves heating water to create steam to rotate the generator.
[15] Data limitations preclude extensive consideration of the situation of older plants subject to rules less stringent than the EPA standards. EPA has prepared data identifying the plants and the applicable rules, but supply analysis is difficult enough without trying to estimate the availability of coal of many different levels of sulfur content.

Table 11 presents the basic data taken from Project Independence estimates. For fossil fuel plants, the data included consist of
the capital outlays per kilowatt of capacity, the non-fuel operating
costs per kilowatt, and heat-rate and utilization-rate assumptions.
For nuclear plants, the capital costs per kilowatt of capacity and all
other costs per kilowatt-hour were used. These were then converted
into estimates of the allowable premium of low-sulfur coal over
high-sulfur coal in coal-fired plants and the allowable prices of different types of coal use competing against nuclear power.[16]

Table 12 summarizes the results of these data manipulations.
First, the total non-fuel costs for the amount of electricity that can
be produced from a million BTUs of coal in a conventional plant are
shown for plants burning high-sulfur coal with scrubbers, plants
burning lignite without scrubbers, and combined-cycle plants using
coal gas.[17] Then the total costs of nuclear power are calculated. This
allows direct calculation of the *premium* that would be paid for
low-sulfur coal that obviates scrubber use and the allowable price of
coal use in conventional boilers when competing against nuclear
power.

The calculations for the combined cycle as a substitute for conventional steam turbines are tedious and inconclusive and will not
be discussed here. The essence of the exercise is that a cheap method
of gasification, low mining costs, and high reliability of the combined
cycle are *all* required to make the combined cycle with coal gas the
preferred alternative to conventional boilers.[18]

Table 13 is designed to allow appraisal of the relative competitive position of eastern and western coal. The data of Table 12 are
combined with the material in Chapter 4 to show the range of

---

[16] The calculations employ a process called levelizing, widely used in the electric-
power-cost literature and explained more fully in Gordon, *U.S. Coal, op. cit.*, pp.
161-68. The present procedure uses the same assumption that a return of 18
percent of the initial investment is required annually to recover the investment
with interest. The required incomes per kilowatt-hour are based on three sets of
assumptions — that the plants operate 75 percent of the time, that they all operate
at the rates FEA specifies for coal plants, and that the coal rates apply to nuclear
plants but combined cycles operate at the lower rates assumed by FEA. The
conversion to cost per million BTUs burned in a conventional coal plant displaced
is based on the FEA estimates of heat rates — the number of BTUs needed to
generate a kilowatt-hour (kwh). The conversion factor, then, is one million divided
by the heat rate, which is the number of kilowatt-hours produced from a million
BTUs.

[17] The table adds calculations for coal plants with scrubbers costing $30 more than
the FEA estimates. This figure was derived from data in the literature suggesting
direct scrubber costs might be as much as $25 above the FEA figures and assuming
the interest during construction on scrubbers had the same ratio to direct scrubber
costs as total interest during construction had to total direct investment costs. The
process of presenting the costs in terms of the amount of electricity generated by a
million BTUs of coal makes the data comparable to coal prices.

[18] The basis of the calculations are explained in Gordon, *U.S. Coal, op. cit.*, pp.
180-82. The complications involve the need to consider the higher thermal
efficiency expected from such combined cycles and the non-coal costs of gasification.

TABLE 11

Project Independence Blueprint Estimates of Electric-Power-Plant Characteristics and Costs, 1980, 1985, and 1990

Characteristic Dimension	High-Sulfur Coal			Lignite			Combined Cycle Using Coal Gas		Nuclear—8 Years' Construction Time			Nuclear—6.5 Years' Construction Time		
	1980	1985	1990	1980	1985	1990	1985	1990	1980	1985	1990	1980	1985	1990
Size (megawatts)	700	800	900	700	800	900	962	1,200	1,000	1,200	1,300	1,100	1,300	1,400
Load factor (percentage)	61	62	63	61	62	63	40	50						
Heat rate (BTU/kwh)	9,175	8,901	8,912	9,175	8,901	8,912	8,300	7,500						
Direct cost of stack gas scrubbers (1974$/kw)	75.00	75.00	75.00											
Total direct environmental control costs (1974$/kw)	102.90	109.90	115.90	14.29	19.68[a]	27.12	12.97	15.78						
Total direct investment (1974$/kw)	306.92	309.59	311.42	268.01	270.13	271.52	164.97	156.78						
Interest during construction (1974$/kw)	70.10	70.75	71.20	61.24	61.72	62.04	24.74	23.52						
Total capital cost (1974$/kw)	377.02	380.34	382.62	329.25	331.85	333.56	189.71	180.30						
First unit (1974$/kw)									478	450	438	440	417	406
Later unit (1974$/kw)									431	408	399	398	379	371
Average (1974$/kw)									455	429	419	419	398	389
General operating cost (mills/kwh)	1.25	1.31	1.38	1.25	1.31	1.38	1.25	1.38	1.00	1.00	1.00	1.00	1.00	1.00
Environmental operating costs (mills/kwh)	4.50	5.05	5.60	1.50	1.75	2.00	1.50	1.65	.15	.15	.15	.15	.15	.15
Fuel-cycle costs (mills/kwh)									2.44	2.82	3.87	2.56	3.52	4.67

[a] Project Independence presents a figure of $43.82, which is far too high relative to the 1980 and 1990 figures, so an interpolated figure was calculated by the author.

Note: Blanks indicate lack of data in the Project Independence Blueprint on the item in question. The volume *Facilities* provides the fossil fuel costs (pp. VII-144-210) and the volume *Nuclear Energy*, the nuclear costs (pp. V-22 and 3.1-8).

Source: U.S. Federal Energy Administration. *Project Independence Blueprint*. Final Task Force Report (Washington: U.S. Government Printing Office, 1974), various volumes.

TABLE 12

Comparative Economics of Alternative Methods of Generating Electricity

(costs in dollars of the amount of electricity generated from a million BTUs of coal in conventional fossil plants, except as noted)

	1980	1985	1990
1. Levelized non-fuel costs of high-sulfur-coal generation:			
a) 75 percent operation; FEA cost assumptions	1.75	1.89	1.96
b) 75 percent operation; costs $30/kw above FEA	1.84	1.98	2.05
c) FEA operating-rate and cost assumptions	2.01	2.13	2.18
d) FEA operating-rate assumptions and costs $30/kw above FEA	2.12	2.24	2.29
2. Levelized non-fuel costs of low-sulfur-coal generation:			
a) 75 percent operation; FEA cost assumptions	1.28	1.37	1.40
b) FEA cost and operating-rate assumptions	1.51	1.58	1.60
3. Levelized non-fuel costs of combined cycle:			
a) 75 percent operation; FEA cost assumptions		0.89	0.89
b) FEA cost and conventional plant-operating-rate assumptions		1.02	1.10
c) FEA cost and combined-cycle operating-rate assumptions		1.40	1.17
4. Levelized total cost of nuclear power:			
a) FEA lower-cost assumption; 75 percent operating rate	1.66	1.75	1.85
b) FEA higher-cost assumption; 75 percent operating rate	1.75	1.77	1.85
c) FEA lower-cost and conventional-coal-plant-operating-rate assumptions	1.94	2.01	2.08
d) FEA higher-cost and conventional-coal-plant-operating-rate assumptions	2.06	2.04	2.10
5. Allowable premium over high-sulfur coal for low-sulfur coal in conventional plant:			
Maximum (1d minus 2a)	.84	.87	.89
Minimum (1a minus 2b)	.24	.31	.36

6. Allowable price of low-sulfur coal in conventional plant compared to nuclear power:			
Maximum (4d minus 2a)	.78	.67	.70
Minimum (4a minus 2b)	.15	.17	.25
7. Allowable price of high-sulfur coal in conventional plant compared to nuclear power:			
Maximum (4d minus 1a)	.31	.15	.14
8. Allowable price per million BTUs of gas in combined cycle in competition with nuclear power:			
Maximum (4d minus 3a adjusted for thermal efficiency)		1.23	1.44
Minimum (4a minus 3c adjusted for thermal efficiency)		.38	.81
9. Allowable coal costs per million BTUs for low-BTU gas in combined cycle in competition with nuclear power:			
Maximum [.82 (8a minus 30 cents)]		.76	.93

Note: The data in this table are derived from Table 11 following the methodology outlined in footnote 16. Annual capital costs are set at 18 percent of total capital costs. The cost per kilowatt-hour is calculated by dividing the annual cost by the number of hours of operation. To this are added the operating costs. To determine the allowable price of coal, the cost per kilowatt-hour is multiplied by the number of kilowatt-hours produced by a million BTUs of coal, calculated by dividing 1,000,000 by the coal-heat rates shown. For example, the first column of 1a is calculated as follows:

$$\begin{array}{ll} \text{Total capital costs} = & \$377.02 \\ \text{times} & \underline{\quad .18} \\ \text{Annual capital costs} = & \underline{\$\ 67.86} \end{array}$$

Given 365 x 24 = 8,760 hours per year, 75 percent operation implies 6,570 hours of operation

$$\begin{array}{ll} \$67.86 \div 6,570 = & \$.01033/\text{kwh} \\ \text{Other operating cost} = & \underline{\$.00575/\text{kwh}} \\ & \underline{\$.01608} \end{array}$$

$$1,000,000 \div 9,175 = 108.99 \text{ kwh/million BTUs}$$
$$\$.01608 \times 108.99 = \$1.75$$

This last step makes these figures dimensionally comparable with coal prices in cents per million BTUs.

transportation cost premiums that can be paid for western coal. These range from 39 cents to $2.39 per million BTUs. Calculations, not shown here, of the actual transportation cost differentials suggest that the allowable premium on western coal is large enough to permit substantial longer-run penetration of the U.S. electric-utility market.[19] However, problems of adapting existing boilers to western coal and the lead times in developing additional producing and transportation facilities for western coal may retard rapid conversion to western coal.

TABLE 13

Range of Freight Premiums Allowable
on Western Coal Competing with Eastern Coal
(cents per millions BTUs)

	Assumptions More Favourable to Eastern Coal			Assumptions Less Favourable to Eastern Coal		
	1980	1985	1990	1980	1985	1990
1. F.o.b. mine price eastern coal (see Table 10)	55	55	55	110	130	165
2. F.o.b. mine price western coal (see Table 10)	30	30	30	15	15	15
3. Eastern coal's cost disadvantage f.o.b. mine (1 minus 2)	15	15	15	95	115	150
4. Eastern coal's cost disadvantage at power plant = premium for low-sulfur fuel (see text)	24	31	36	84	87	89
5. Allowable transportation cost premium (3 plus 4) on western coal	39	46	51	179	202	239

Note: The favourable and unfavourable coal prices come from Table 10; the cost disadvantages come from Table 12. The more favourable assumptions involve the lower eastern coal price, the higher western coal price, and the lower estimate of the premium for low-sulfur fuel; the less favourable assumptions are the exact opposite in each case.

---

[19] The different BTU content in eastern and western coal complicates the analysis in a fashion that precludes a simple discussion of the transportation rate differential. A given rate per ton translates into a lower rate per million BTUs for a high-BTU coal. This advantage increases with distance. For example, assuming a two-cent-per-ton-mile transportation charge, 24-million-BTUs-per-ton eastern coal, and 16-million-BTUs-per-ton western coal, it would cost 75 cents per million BTUs to move western coal 600 miles; it would cost 8.3 cents to move eastern coal 100 miles — a 67-cent advantage. When distances rise to 1,500 and 1,400 miles, respectively, the costs rise to $1.88 and $1.17 for a differential of 71 cents. The calulations show that the assumptions less favourable to eastern coal imply that whether transportation rates are one or two cents per ton-mile, western coal will indeed be the cheaper fuel throughout most of the United States. Eastern coal prices at the low end of my range are required to offset substantial western coal penetration of eastern markets.

Coal's Competitive Position

The data on delivered prices in Table 14 indicate that eastern coal is unlikely to be competitive with nuclear power but that western coal might compete in markets less than 1,000 miles from the coal fields. (Those who feel the figures presented here understate the cost of nuclear plants may use a rough rule of thumb — every $100 increase in capital cost is equivalent to a rise of 35 cents in the cost of the amount of electricity generated by a million BTUs of coal — to adjust the present figures.) Similarly, I can conclude that the combined cycle using coal gas does not radically improve the position of coal compared to nuclear power.

The essence of these calculations is that the U.S. coal industry east of the Mississippi faces a severe long-run loss of competitive position. Nuclear power, or perhaps western coal, is likely to take over the electric-utility market. As already noted, enormous uncertainties exist about both the accuracy of this prognosis and the time path that will be followed.

It may be noted parenthetically that these data also suggest that even current oil prices may not be high enough to make coal competitive on a pure cost basis. Low-sulfur fuel oil was being delivered in early 1975 to East Coast utilities for prices of around $2.00 per million BTUs. Expensive eastern coal and high emission-control costs could easily produce eastern coal costs well above $2.00 per million BTUs in much of the eastern United States (Table 12 indicates emission-control costs could exceed 80 cents per million BTUs, and Table 13 shows that f.o.b. mine prices in the 1980s could exceed $1.00 per million BTUs with appropriately higher delivered prices). Similarly, the worst assumptions about western coal suggest it could not compete with $2.00-per-million-BTU oil in eastern markets.

At this point it may be appropriate to indicate the further implications of these data on coal and to introduce some comparisons between synthetic crude oil and methane from coal and other fuel alternatives. As noted, anyone who uses fuels essentially for heat faces the same basic problems as an electric utility, and if the fuel use is on a sufficiently large scale, any of the expedients available to electric utilities can be adopted. However, many of the alternatives are likely to be prohibitively expensive for small-scale consumers of energy.

Thus one can expect a spectrum of consumers ranging from those who will have wide choices to those who will be limited to methane, fuel oil, and electricity. There is no simple way to relate any of the prior analysis to cover all these cases. Such a review would lead us into precisely the complications that Chapter 1 indicated were beyond the scope of this study.

TABLE 14

Sample Delivered Prices of Eastern and Western Coal[a]
(cents per million BTUs)

	Optimistic[b] Eastern	Pessimistic Eastern			Optimistic[b] Western	Pessimistic[c] Western
		1980	1985	1990		
F.o.b. mine price (see Table 10)	55	110	130	165	15	30
plus 100 miles freight	59	118	138	173	21	43
200 miles freight	63	127	147	182	28	55
300 miles freight	68	135	155	190	34	68
400 miles freight	72	143	163	198	40	80
500 miles freight	76	152	172	207	46	93
600 miles freight	80	160	180	215	53	105
700 miles freight	84	168	188	223	58	118
800 miles freight	88	177	197	232	65	130
900 miles freight	92	185	205	240	71	143
1,000 miles freight	96	193	213	248	78	155
1,100 miles freight	100	202	222	257	84	168
1,200 miles freight	104	210	230	265	90	180
1,300 miles freight	108	218	238	273	96	193
1,400 miles freight	112	227	247	282	103	205
1,500 miles freight	117	235	255	290	109	218

[a] Eastern coal, 24 million BTUs per ton; western coal, 16 million BTUs per ton.
[b] Optimistic forecast, 1 cent per ton-mile.
[c] Pessimistic rate, 2 cents per ton-mile.

For example, it is extremely difficult even to place electric-power-generating cost estimates given here and figures that have appeared on the costs of synthetic fuels from coal and oil shale on a dimensionally comparable basis. Adjustments must be made for transportation costs, further processing requirements, and differences in the cost of the equipment in which the fuel is used. To give a rough idea of the possibilities, Table 15 compares Energy Research and Development Agency (ERDA) estimates of the required selling price of crude oil from oil shale to those of synthetic crude oil and methane from western coal. The figures on the sources of synthetic crude oil are the most closely comparable figures that can be easily generated from the available data. Crude oil from western coal and shale would be closely competitive and, if produced near the coal or shale (as these figures assume), would have similar locational positions relative to major markets. The data show that oil from shale is markedly cheaper than liquid fuel from coal. Thus oil from shale represents formidable potential competition for oil from coal. (Of course, if processing has to be conducted at locations remote from the mining, shale's position could rapidly deteriorate, since much more shale material would have to be shipped than coal.)

TABLE 15

ERDA 1975 Estimates of Synthetic-Fuel Costs
(cents per million BTUs)

	Rates of Return			Regulated Rate
	12%	15%	20%	of Return[a]
High BTU gas:				
Coal at 29 cents/million BTUs	3.69	4.43	5.89	2.61
Coal at 46 cents/million BTUs	3.99	4.73	6.19	2.91
Coal at 53 cents/million BTUs	4.12	4.84	6.27	3.02
Coal at 71 cents/million BTUs	4.44	5.16	6.59	3.34
Synthetic crude oil from coal:				
Coal at 29 cents/million BTUs	2.89	3.45	4.60	2.05
Coal at 46 cents/million BTUs	3.15	3.71	4.86	2.31
Coal at 53 cents/million BTUs	3.26	3.82	4.97	2.42
Coal at 71 cents/million BTUs	3.53	4.10	5.22	2.70
Crude oil from oil shale	1.62	2.03	2.87	n.a.

n.a. = not applicable.

[a] Set at allowing 15 percent return on equity investment as calculated by a regulatory agency and assuming financing by 75 percent debt and 25 percent equity.

Source: The data in this table are derived from U.S. Synfuels Interagency Task Force, *Recommendations for a Synthetic Fuels Commercialization Program*, Vol. 3, pp. 1-5, 1-29, and 1-30.

As for the cost estimates for gas, the implications are less clear-cut, but in many respects they do indicate that the gas would clearly be uncompetitive with heavy fuel oil from shale. Such heavy fuel oil from shale would sell for less than the crude (otherwise crude would be burned directly), and oil is cheaper to transport than gas. It would similarly appear that the higher transportation and production costs of synthetic methane from coal are likely to outweigh the tendency of lighter fuel oils to sell for more than crude oil. Thus in addition to the competitive pressures from electricity and oil and gas from conventional sources, synthetic fuels from coal face significant competitive pressures from oil shale.

Electricity Markets in Canada

Comparably detailed cost estimates do not appear to be available for Canada, but extensive information exists on the general trends in electric-utility fuel use. Basically, I consider two distinct electric-utility markets — one fairly well assured for local coal in the western coal-mining provinces, principally Alberta and Saskatchewan, and one of uncertain magnitude in Ontario. The western provinces have already begun the use of subbituminous (in Alberta) and lignite (in Saskatchewan), with consumption of around six million and three million tons, respectively, in 1974. Alberta, at least, has formulated a program of coal consumption through the year 2001. By 2001, electricity generation in Alberta is expected to consume 55 million tons of coal per year.

(The government of Alberta notes that this will accumulate to 719 million tons of consumption from 1972 to 2001 and that the plants installed through 2001 will use a further 946 million tons their remaining useful life — i.e., until the year 2031. The post-2001 additions to capacity are expected to be in the form of nuclear power. As noted in Chapter 3, the province is concerned that these demands, combined with expected sales to other regions, might lead to severe depletion of strip-mineable resources and wants future grants of mining rights controlled to preserve these supplies for its own use.)

The Ontario situation is much more complicated. Starting in the early fifties, Ontario Hydro began adding coal-fired capacity to its system, with total coal consumption remaining modest through 1961 (when it reached 272,000 tons). The next year coal use jumped to 1.5 million tons and then climbed steadily, to 9.4 million tons in 1971 and 1972. Heavy use of nuclear plants caused drops in coal use in 1973 and 1974. (Use in 1974 was about 6 million tons.)

All of Ontario Hydro's coal-burning capacity has been designed to use 26-million-BTU-per-ton U.S. coal, and it will not be until the 1980s that plants designed to burn lignite or subbituminous can be added in substantial amounts.[20] Given the problems of boiler con-

[20] Two 150-megawatt units designed to burn lignite are planned for Thunder Bay, one in 1979 and the other in 1980. Other fossil-fired additions to current capacity through to 1980 will consist of 2,000 megawatts of capacity designed to burn U.S. coal and 4,295 megawatts designed to burn oil. During the 1982-87 period Ontario

(Cont'd on page 63)

version, concern over the workability of scrubbers, the underlying economics, and a long-term commitment to emphasis on nuclear power, Ontario Hydro does not consider a massive shift to lignite or subbituminous a satisfactory solution, at least in the short run. Its preferred strategy for meeting pollution requirements is to purchase 22-million-BTU-per-ton low-sulfur coal in western Canada for blending with U.S. coal. Such blends burn much more satisfactorily than subbituminous and lignite and still meet air-pollution standards.

On the basis of this strategy and of forecasts made early in 1975, Ontario Hydro has indicated that by 1979 the use of U.S. coal will rise to 12 million tons (double the 1974 consumption rate), supplemented by Canadian bituminous coal equivalent in heat value to 5.9 million tons of U.S. bituminous. The consumption of U.S. coal will then remain steady well into the later 1980s, with Canadian bituminous supplying the additional requirements.

The choice of western Canadian bituminous as the incremental source of low-sulfur coal has been justified as a means of diversifying fuel supplies to reduce sensitivity to developments in one area. Just what the economic implication of this rationale will be is quite unclear. Ontario Hydro can certainly use the arguments made above to argue that western Canadian coal is likely to be cheaper in the long run than low-sulfur Appalachian coal. Given estimated f.o.b. mine costs of $13-18 per ton and transportation costs of $20-23, Canadian low-sulfur bituminous would cost $33-41 per ton delivered. Ontario Hydro believes that it currently can secure low-sulfur U.S. coal at a delivered price of about $35 per ton or $1.45 per million BTUs, which is less than the *minimum* expected delivered costs of $1.50 per million BTUs of Canadian coal. However, with costs expected to escalate in underground mining because of poor productivity, this advantage for U.S. coal could be eroded.

There are two possible problems with this approach — neglect of low-sulfur, underground-mined bituminous in Utah and conservatism over boiler modification. Present mining costs in Utah probably are no higher than in western Canada, and transportation costs would be significantly lower. Offsetting these advantages are uncertainties about how easily supply can be expanded in Utah and the political impacts of substantial foreign purchases. (The thought of modest shipments to Japan created a furor in the western United States, and similar problems might arise with Utah coal, even though no strip-mining problems are involved.) Given the mixed

(Cont'd from page 62)

Hydro has scheduled capacity increases of 3,600 megawatts using lignite or subbituminous coal. Finally, although Ontario Hydro has not produced cost studies on the CANDU reactor as detailed as those made for U.S. reactors, a 1975 estimate suggests that a CANDU reactor is competitive with a coal-fired generator using 60-cent-per-million-BTU coal (see H. A. Smith, *A Review of the Development and Status of CANDU Nuclear Power Plant* [Toronto: Ontario Hydro, 1975]; this is one of three separately paged papers bound together in the report).

experience of U.S. utilities with western coal, Ontario Hydro may have good reason to fear shifting to subbituminous or lignite.

In short, Ontario Hydro expects to continue increasing its use of U.S. coal. It further intends to retain its policy of covering its needs through long-term contracts. Thus it promises to be a modest, predictable, and stable influence on the U.S. coal market.

Uncertain Outlook for Coking Coal

The coking coal situation is even more ambiguous. In the years to, say, 1985, the basic economic issue is the comparative mining economy of Appalachian and western Canadian metallurgical coal. The uncertainties affecting western Canada have already been noted; the situation for Appalachia can be summed up by noting that the metallurgical coal producers have all the problems of steam coal producers plus the additional one of possibly greater depletion of the best resources. Thus the comparative development of the two suppliers is difficult to predict. The available evidence suggests that Canadian steel companies who secure substantial amounts of their coal from mines they own in the United States will continue to use U.S. coal for an extended period and will move relatively timidly towards use of western Canadian coal. The move may, indeed, be so slow and timid that by that time possible radical changes in steel industry fuel-use technology will have proved viable.

Two developments are particularly critical. First, fears of rising costs of the coal traditionally used in coke manufacture and difficulties in controlling air pollution from coke ovens have inspired research on new coking techniques. Such techniques would simultaneously broaden the range of types of usable coal and have lesser pollution-control problems. Second, much interest has arisen in new, "direct reduction" processes, which produce iron without the use of coke. Actually, the technique most frequently discussed is an extension of a processing approach already well-established in the steel industry — iron ore pelletizing. Pelletizing involves pretreating ores to remove substantial amounts of waste prior to processing the material in the blast furnace, reducing the work and coke needed in the blast furnace. A process called double reduction, which yields a high degree of purification, is considered promising as producing both an even better, lower-coke-using feed for blast furnaces and a material that can be directly used in electric steel-making furnaces, bypassing the blast furnace altogether. In any case, of course, the prereduction substitutes other sources of energy for coke.

The new coking techniques are still in the development stage, but projects to produce and utilize double-reduced pellets have already been instituted. Nevertheless, it will be at least the late 1980s before either technique will become a major influence. Thus there are uncertainties about where the problems of coking coal supplies will be most severe in the next decade and whether technical advances will lessen the concern in the long run by widening the coal-use choices of the steel industry.

Summing Up

The long-run prospects for coal in existing markets, let alone in markets currently supplied by other fossil fuels, remain quite unclear at this time. Steam coal, traditionally used to generate electricity in Ontario and in the eastern United States, will be faced with a challenge from nuclear power. Even oil shale, which many believe to be a high-risk alternative to crude oil and gas in the future, also poses a long-term threat to coal markets. Moreover, the conversion of coal into synthetic substitutes needs greater investigation before anything can be said about its future. Finally, the use of coal for coking purposes is in the process of being radically altered as new technology tries to reduce the role of coal in the production of steel.

A crowning irony of the post-1973 interest in new energy sources is that it has created mounting difficulties in reaching accord over the prospects of different energy alternatives. Clearly, then, this is hardly the time to make firm plans for future fuel use; it is the time for calm and rational discussions on coal policy.

6

Coal and the Future of
Canada-U.S. Energy Relations

With the prospects for a major revival in the use of coal as an alternative energy source, particularly in the United States, still in some considerable doubt, can I say anything specific about future coal developments and their implications for Canada-U.S. energy relations? Does Canada have legitimate reasons to fear a U.S. export embargo, and if so, what does this mean for the exchange of other forms of energy such as oil, gas, electricity, and possibly uranium? These and other questions are examined in this final chapter, in which I conclude that only a complete breakdown of bilateral energy relations would precipitate U.S. action to deny Canada coal supplies.

Before turning to these issues, it is useful to restate my main findings regarding the outlook for coal in the next decade or more.

Until well into the 1980s, the United States will probably be using an increasing amount of coal — primarily in the present consuming sectors of electric utilities and metallurgical coke manufacture. This conclusion is based on the dual assumptions that other domestic alternatives cannot be developed quickly enough to displace coal and that resistance to heavily increased oil imports (combined with considerable logistics problems of transporting imported oil to inland power plants) will remain intense. Whatever the true economic attractiveness of domestic oil, gas, and nuclear power as alternatives to coal, the technical lead times in their development are too long for massive contributions to occur until the early or middle 1980s. Moreover, substantial further delays are being imposed by public policy restraints, such as the long delays in leasing the Atlantic Outer Continental Shelf.

On the other hand, it should not be inferred that an expansion of coal production is assured, given the long delays that occur in developing new domestic sources of fossil fuel and nuclear power. Here, again, U.S. public policy is causing longer delays in the exploitation of coal reserves. For example, pressures are being exerted for the rapid implementation of stringent air-pollution standards and the imposition of severe restraints on the strip-mining of low-sulfur western coal. Given the present state of alternative pollution-control options, such as stack gas scrubbing, it is doubtful that an increase in coal use can be attained without either delaying the schedules for attaining some environmental goals or easing present restrictions on western coal development. Thus the forecast of increased coal use is conditional on public policy changes to produce more gradual timetables for the implementation of federal air-pollution standards, state restraint from seeking cleaner ambient air than federal standards (including those of non-degradation) require, and some resolution of the blockages to leasing of western coal lands.

Another series of caveats relates to the desirability of this commitment to coal. Leaving aside for the moment appraisal of past actions that contributed to the pressures, we must still note that the devotion to reduced oil import growth may be excessive, and some might argue that the problems of oil imports are less than those of air pollution and disruption of the West. Moreover, while the past, of course, cannot be reversed, it should be noted that there are those who implicitly believe that the need to increase coal use substantially could have been avoided. Among these are the people cited in Chapter 1 who believe that the rise in world oil prices could have been prevented and those who feel that the development of nuclear energy was unduly retarded.

In any event, growth in coal consumption will probably be accompanied by a massive relocation of the industry, which will undoubtedly be accompanied by delays in, and disruptions of, production schedules. It will take considerable time, for example, to build up a well-trained and highly motivated work force in new producing areas, especially in regions like the Great Plains, where labour is already in scarce supply. Also, the putting into place of mining machinery and equipment and the improvement of existing transportation lines, let alone the construction of new facilities, are all part of the cost, in terms of both time and resources, that the industry must undergo in the relocation process as it tries to adjust its production to meet future growth.

In general, the longer-run prospects for a substantial shift towards greater use of coal in the United States must be viewed with considerable skepticism. For one thing, the emergence of nuclear power may well push coal aside in the electric-power industry, currently coal's biggest market. For another, several obstacles still stand in the way of the creation of an economically viable synthetic-fuel industry to replace diminishing domestic supplies of crude oil and natural gas. Moreover, it will be even more likely that, whatever the behaviour of coal demand, marketing patterns will change radically, although the precise nature of this change remains very uncertain at this early date. Specifically, not only can we expect a movement towards the development of western coal, but new coking methods may greatly broaden the range of coal acceptable for coke making, and new iron-making techniques may lessen the need for coke. In short, there are far too many questions that need to be answered before we can confidently forecast a massive swing towards greater consumption of coal in the United States.

With these considerations in mind, we can turn to the longer- and shorter-run aspects of the availability of U.S. coal to Canada. Every indication suggests that in the longer run (i.e., from the late 1980s on), developments in the coal market are unlikely to create unmanageable problems for Canada in securing U.S. coal. A westward shift of U.S. steam coal production should ease any pressure on eastern mines, and new technologies in the steel industry should make access to metallurgical coal in Appalachia at least as great as it is today.

The probability of an embargo or a tightening of supply in the interim period is less easy to dismiss, but by no means a serious threat. Clearly, the exports to Ontario Hydro by themselves are not a particularly likely target for control, for Ontario Hydro is essentially absorbing only a small fraction of the steam coal production of Appalachia, and sequestering the coal for U.S. use would have no measurable impact on coal supplies.

It is the metallurgical coal exports of the United States that could conceivably be a target of any embargo, since the diversion of this coal could, in principle, make a major contribution to increasing the supply of low-sulfur coal to eastern U.S. customers. A number of forces would, however, operate to limit the pressures for such an embargo with respect to both its imposition and its enforcement. First, some metallurgical coals may not be particularly suited for combustion in existing boilers. Second, it is not clear that a strong enough consensus for an embargo could be developed. Even those most likely to propose embargoes — the electric utilities, the steel industry, and the Environmental Protection Agency — may find it expedient to restrain their advocacy. The utilities might antagonize their customers and suppliers by their vigorous support of an embargo and would also have difficulty explaining away past assertions that metallurgical coal was too valuable to use in utility boilers. EPA would similarly have difficulties explaining why it had waited so long to determine the need for the coal.

Moreover, Canada possesses the ability for meaningful retaliation should the United States impose supply restrictions on its coal exports. U.S. electric utilities rely heavily on interconnections with their Canadian counterparts in several provinces besides Ontario for extra power at peak demand periods. In addition, U.S. steel companies would be unlikely to support an embargo or supply restraint for fear that Canada would do the same on its shipments of iron ore south of the border. An interesting side issue is how the peculiar importance of Canada as an iron and nickel supplier to the United States would affect the implementation of an embargo. In particular, it could be conjectured that some form of favouritism might exempt Canada from such countermeasures. The prospects for a Canadian exemption would be very good in the cases of informal controls, where there would be an opportunity for some sort of bilateral agreement to be worked out.

As far as a simple tightening of the coking coal market is concerned, this seems a problem the steel industry can solve by itself. The lead times on new mines are sufficiently long, and the alternatives sufficiently broad (i.e., there are many non-U.S. sources of supply), that the need for adaptations should be recognized and action be taken in a timely fashion.

Finally, opposition to an embargo would be vigorously expressed by exporting coal companies and the U.S. State Department. Moreover, given the existence of long-term contracts, and even ownership interests, importers of U.S. coal would undoubtedly sue to block an embargo. This would surely produce severe delays and, quite possibly, permanent blockage to export embargoes.

This does not mean that supplies of U.S. coal to Canada can be considered assured; rather it can be concluded that a cutoff would not be due to the impact of the coal purchases by themselves. The disruptions would more likely result from a general breakdown in U.S.-Canadian energy relationships or a general coal-export-embargo policy. Either step would cause repercussions of so profound a nature that they seem most unlikely. The strong degree of economic interdependence between the United States and its major coal customers is such that outright coal embargoes are improbable. Even if domestic pressures to limit surges of coal exports became irresistible, it seems likely that the past U.S. pattern of ad hoc, often informal, controls, such as were applied to lumber and soybean exports and textile, steel, and Canadian oil imports, would be employed. In such a system, one would expect regular buyers to be favoured over spot purchasers.

A breakdown in U.S.-Canadian energy relations appears too catastrophic an event for either government to permit its happening. The range of present and potential energy interdependence — possible U.S. access to Canadian Arctic oil and gas, the right to build pipelines from Alaska through Canada, the interchange of electricity between the countries, and Canada's reliance on U.S. coal and pipelines in the United States — is, by itself, simply too great to permit a breakdown. Moreover, the broader interdependence between the two economies reinforces the need for avoiding severe discord over energy. It may be recalled that the two U.S. industries most likely to pressure for coal export controls have a particularly great interest in preserving good economic ties with Canada. The U.S. steel industry relies heavily on Canadian iron ore and nickel; the electric-power industry imports more power from Canada than it exports. Thus, whatever the future of coal, it is generally unlikely that it will affect, or be affected greatly by, crises in U.S.-Canadian relationships.

R. L. Adams:

While I have signed this transmittal statement believing that the author's views merit publication, I cannot endorse his research findings, as I believe his conclusions are invalid (i.e., significantly expanded coal production is improbable, and coal will not be competitive with oil, gas, or nuclear fuels).

Robert Blair:

I must register my dissent with the findings regarding the prospects of converting coal into synthetic oil and gas. The report makes judgments based on the present technology, which implies a downgrading of the potential for advances in coal technology. As a result, the Committee statement tends to assign a low value to coal conversion even in the future, and this may discourage current large-scale efforts to develop what could be one of several attractive energy options in the 1980s and beyond.

Thomas E. Covel:

This report makes a useful contribution to public understanding of the prospects regarding coal, and I am pleased to sign the transmittal statement, but with one reservation. It seems to me that the author's forecast of future Canadian-American energy relations on page 66 may be logical, but it is frightening in its implications of such possible deterioration. I believe a more cooperative spirit can and will exist.

MEMBERS OF THE CANADIAN-AMERICAN COMMITTEE

Co-Chairmen

ROBERT M. MacINTOSH
Executive Vice-President,
The Bank of Nova Scotia,
Toronto, Ontario

RICHARD J. SCHMEELK
Partner, Salomon Brothers,
New York, New York

Members

I. W. ABEL
President, United Steelworkers of America,
AFL-CIO, Pittsburgh, Pennsylvania

JOHN N. ABELL
Vice President and Director, Wood Gundy
Limited, Toronto, Ontario

R. L. ADAMS
Executive Vice President, Continental Oil
Company, Stamford, Connecticut

J. A. ARMSTRONG
President and Chief Executive Officer, Imperial Oil Limited, Toronto, Ontario

IAN A. BARCLAY
Chairman and Chief Executive Officer,
British Columbia Forest Products Limited,
Vancouver, British Columbia

MICHEL BELANGER
President, Provincial Bank of Canada,
Montreal, Quebec

ROY F. BENNETT
President and Chief Executive Officer, Ford
Motor Company of Canada, Limited, Oak-
ville, Ontario

ROD J. BILODEAU
Chairman of the Board, Honeywell Limited,
Scarborough, Ontario

ROBERT BLAIR
President and Chief Executive Officer, Al-
berta Gas Trunk Line Company Limited,
Calgary, Alberta

BART H. BOSSIDY
Group Vice President — International Fib-
ers, Celanese Corporation, New York, New
York

J. E. BRENT
Chairman of the Board, IBM Canada Ltd.,
Toronto, Ontario

PHILIP BRIGGS
Senior Vice President, Metropolitan Life Insurance Company, New York, New York

ARDEN BURBIDGE
Burbidge Farm, Park River, North Dakota

NICHOLAS J. CAMPBELL, JR.
Director and Senior Vice President, Exxon
Corporation, New York, New York

SHIRLEY CARR
Executive Vice-President, Canadian Labour
Congress, Ottawa, Ontario

W. R. CLERIHUE
Executive Vice-President, Staff and Adminis-
tration, Celanese Corporation, New York,
New York

HON. JOHN V. CLYNE
MacMillan Bloedel Limited, Vancouver,
British Columbia

STANTON R. COOK
President, Tribune Company, Chicago, Illinois

THOMAS E. COVEL
Marion, Massachusetts

GEORGE B. CURRIE
Vancouver, British Columbia

RAYMOND L. DAVIS
International Trade Affairs Representative,
National Association of Wheat Growers, Pot-
ter, Nebraska

J. S. DEWAR
President, Union Carbide Canada Limited,
Toronto, Ontario

JOHN H. DICKEY
President, Nova Scotia Pulp Limited,
Halifax, Nova Scotia

JOHN S. DICKEY
President Emeritus and Bicentennial Pro-
fessor of Public Affairs, Dartmouth College,
Hanover, New Hampshire

THOMAS W. diZEREGA
Vice President, Northwest Pipeline Corporation, Salt Lake City, Utah

WILLIAM DODGE
Ottawa, Ontario

A. D. DUNTON
Professor and Director, Institute of Canadian
Studies, Carleton University, Ottawa, On-
tario

STEPHEN C. EYRE
Comptroller, First National City Bank, New
York, New York

A. J. FISHER
President, Fiberglas Canada Limited, Toronto, Ontario

CHARLES F. FOGARTY
Chairman and Chief Executive Officer,
Texasgulf Inc., New York, New York

MEMBERS 73

ROBERT M. FOWLER
President, C. D. Howe Research Institute,
Montreal, Quebec

JOHN F. GALLAGHER
Vice President, International Operations,
Sears, Roebuck and Company, Chicago, Illinois

CARL J. GILBERT
Dover, Massachusetts

WAYNE E. GLENN
Vice Chairman, Continental Oil Company,
Stamford, Connecticut

DONALD R. GRANGAARD
President, First Bank System, Inc., Minneapolis, Minnesota

PAT GREATHOUSE
Vice President, International Union, UAW,
Detroit, Michigan

A.D. HAMILTON
President and Chief Executive Officer, Domtar Limited, Montreal, Quebec

JOHN A. HANNAH
Dansville, Michigan

ROBERT H. HANSEN
Group Vice-President, Avon Products, Inc.,
New York, New York

F. PEAVEY HEFFELFINGER
Director Emeritus, Peavey Company, Minneapolis, Minnesota

R. A. IRWIN
Chairman, Consolidated-Bathurst Limited,
Montreal, Quebec

EDGAR F. KAISER, JR.
President and Chief Executive Officer, Kaiser
Resources Ltd., Vancouver, British Columbia

JOSEPH D. KEENAN
International Secretary, International
Brotherhood of Electrical Workers, AFL-CIO,
Washington, D.C.

DONALD P. KELLY
President and Chief Operating Officer, Esmark, Inc., Chicago, Illinois

DAVID KIRK
Executive Secretary, The Canadian Federation of Agriculture, Ottawa, Ontario

LANE KIRKLAND
Secretary-Treasurer, AFL-CIO, Washington,
D.C.

WILLIAM J. KUHFUSS
Mackinaw, Illinois

J. L. KUHN
President and General Manager, 3M Canada
Limited, London, Ontario

HERBERT H. LANK
Director, Du Pont of Canada Limited,
Montreal, Quebec

PAUL LEMAN
President, Alcan Aluminium Limited,
Montreal, Quebec

EDMOND A. LEMIEUX
General Manager — Finance, Hydro-Quebec,
Montreal, Quebec

FRANKLIN A. LINDSAY
Chairman, Itek Corporation, Lexington, Massachusetts

L. H. LORRAIN
President, Canadian Paperworkers Union,
Montreal, Quebec

WILBER H. MACK
Chairman and Chief Executive Officer,
American Natural Gas Company, Detroit,
Michigan

M. W. MACKENZIE
Vice Chairman, Canron Limited, Montreal,
Quebec

WILLIAM MAHONEY
National Director, United Steelworkers of
America, AFL-CIO-CLC, Toronto, Ontario

JULIEN MAJOR
Executive Vice-President, Canadian Labour
Congress, Ottawa, Ontario

PAUL M. MARSHALL
President, Canadian Hydrocarbons Ltd., Calgary, Alberta

FRANCIS L. MASON
Senior Vice President, The Chase Manhattan
Bank, New York, New York

DENNIS McDERMOTT
UAW International Vice President and Director for Canada, International Union,
UAW of America, Willowdale, Ontario

WILLIAM J. McDONOUGH
Executive Vice President, The First National
Bank of Chicago, Chicago, Illinois

WILLIAM C. Y. McGREGOR
International Vice President, Brotherhood of
Railway, Airline and Steamship Clerks,
Montreal, Quebec

H. WALLACE MERRYMAN
Chairman and Chief Executive Officer, Avco
Financial Services, Inc., Newport Beach,
California

JOHN MILLER
President, National Planning Association,
Washington, D.C.

COLMAN M. MOCKLER, JR.
Chairman and President, The Gillette Company, Boston, Massachusetts

DONALD R. MONTGOMERY
Secretary-Treasurer, Canadian Labour Congress, Ottawa, Ontario

JOSEPH MORRIS
President, Canadian Labour Congress, Ottawa, Ontario

0# 74 MEMBERS

RICHARD W. MUZZY
Vice President—International, Owens-Corning Fiberglas Corporation, Toledo, Ohio

THEODORE NELSON
Executive Vice President, Mobil Oil Corporation, New York, New York

THOMAS S. NICHOLS, SR.
Director, Olin Corporation, New York, New York

CARL E. NICKELS, JR.
Vice President, Finance and Administration, The Hanna Mining Company, Cleveland, Ohio

JOSEPH E. NOLAN
President and Trustee, Weyerhaeuser Company Foundation, Tacoma, Washington

HON. VICTOR deB. OLAND
Halifax, Nova Scotia

CHARLES PERRAULT
President, Perconsult Ltd., Montreal, Quebec

RICHARD H. PETERSON
Vice Chairman of the Board, Pacific Gas and Electric Company, San Francisco, California

BEN L. ROUSE
Vice-President — International Group, Burroughs Corporation, Detroit, Michigan

HENRY E. RUSSELL
President, Boston Safe Deposit and Trust Company, Boston, Massachusetts

THOMAS W. RUSSELL, JR.
Senior Vice President, Haley Associates, Inc., New York, New York

A. E. SAFARIAN
Dean, School of Graduate Studies, University of Toronto, Toronto, Ontario

W. B. SAUNDERS
Group Vice President, Cargill, Incorporated, Minneapolis, Minnesota

HON. ADOLPH W. SCHMIDT
Ligonier, Pennsylvania

A. R. SLOAN
President and General Manager, Continental Can International, Stamford, Connecticut

EDSON W. SPENCER
President and Chief Executive Officer, Honeywell Inc., Minneapolis, Minnesota

W. A. STRAUSS
Chairman and President, Northern Natural Gas Company, Omaha, Nebraska

ROBERT D. STUART, JR.
President, The Quaker Oats Company, Chicago, Illinois

A. McC. SUTHERLAND
Senior Vice President, The International Nickel Company of Canada, Limited, Toronto, Ontario

DWIGHT D. TAYLOR
Senior Vice President, Crown Zellerbach Corporation, San Francisco, California

ROBERT B. TAYLOR
Chairman, Ontario Hydro, Toronto, Ontario

E. K. TURNER
President, Saskatchewan Wheat Pool, Regina, Saskatchewan

WILLIAM I. M. TURNER, JR.
President and Chief Executive Officer, Consolidated-Bathurst Limited, Montreal, Quebec

W. O. TWAITS
Toronto, Ontario

MELVIN J. WERNER
Vice President, Farmers Union Grain Terminal Association, Saint Paul, Minnesota

JOHN R. WHITE
New York, New York

HENRY S. WINGATE
Formerly Chairman and Chief Officer, The International Nickel Company of Canada, Ltd., New York, New York

WILLIAM W. WINPISINGER
General Vice President, International Association of Machinists and Aerospace Workers, Washington, D.C.

THOMAS WINSHIP
Editor, *Boston Globe*, Boston, Massachusetts

FRANCIS G. WINSPEAR
Edmonton, Alberta

D. MICHAEL WINTON
Chairman, Pas Lumber Company Limited, Minneapolis, Minnesota

GEORGE W. WOODS
President, TransCanada Pipelines, Toronto, Ontario

WILLIAM S. WOODSIDE
President, American Can Company, Greenwich, Connecticut

ADAM H. ZIMMERMAN
Executive Vice President, Noranda Mines Limited, Toronto, Ontario

Honorary Members

EDWARD F. BLETTNER
Honorary Director, The First National Bank of Chicago, Chicago, Illinois

HON. N. A. M. MacKENZIE
Vancouver, British Columbia

HAROLD SWEATT
Honorary Chairman of the Board, Honeywell Inc., Minneapolis, Minnesota

DAVID J. WINTON
Minneapolis, Minnesota

SELECTED PUBLICATIONS
OF THE CANADIAN-AMERICAN COMMITTEE*

Commercial Relations

CAC-40 *Industrial Incentive Policies and Programs in the Canadian-American Context,* by John Volpe. 1976 ($2.50)

CAC-38 *A Balance of Payments Handbook,* by Caroline Pestieau. 1974 ($2.00)

CAC-32 *Toward a More Realistic Appraisal of the Automotive Agreement,* a Statement by the Committee. 1970 ($1.00)

CAC-31 *The Canada-U.S. Automotive Agreement: An Evaluation,* by Carl E. Beigie. 1970 ($3.00)

CAC-27 *Constructive Alternatives to Proposals for U.S. Import Quotas,* a Statement by the Committee. 1968 ($1.00)

CAC-25 *A New Trade Strategy for Canada and the United States,* a Statement by the Committee. 1966 ($1.00)

CAC-23 *A Possible Plan for a Canada-U.S. Free Trade Area,* a Staff Report. 1965 ($1.50)

CAC-21 *A Canada-U.S. Free Trade Arrangement: Survey of Possible Characteristics,* by Sperry Lea. 1963 ($2.00)

Energy and Other Resources

CAC-41 *Coal and Canada-U.S. Energy Relations,* by Richard L. Gordon. 1976 ($3.00)

CAC-39 *Keeping Options Open in Canada-U.S. Oil and Natural Gas Trade,* a Statement by the Committee. 1975 ($1.00)

CAC-37 *Canada, the United States, and the Third Law of the Sea Conference,* by R. M. Logan. 1974 ($3.00)

CAC-36 *Energy from the Arctic: Facts and Issues,* by Judith Maxwell. 1973 ($4.00)

Investment

CAC-33 *Canada's Experience with Fixed and Flexible Exchange Rates in a North-American Capital Market,* by Robert M. Dunn, Jr. 1971 ($2.00)

CAC-29 *The Performance of Foreign-Owned Firms in Canada,* by A.E. Safarian. 1969 ($2.00)

CAC-24 *Capital Flows Between Canada and the United States,* by Irving Brecher. 1965 ($2.00)

---

*These and other Committee publications may be ordered from the Committee's offices at 2064 Sun Life Building, Montreal, Quebec H3B 2X7, and at 1606 New Hampshire Avenue, N.W., Washington, D. C. 20009. Quantity discounts are given. A Descriptive flyer of these publications is also available.

SPONSORING ORGANIZATIONS

The C. D. Howe Research Institute is a private, non-political, non-profit organization founded in January, 1973, by the merger of the C. D. Howe Memorial Foundation and the Private Planning Association of Canada, to undertake research into Canadian economic policy issues, especially in the areas of international policy and major government programs.

HRI continues the activities of the PPAC. These include the work of three established committees, composed of agricultural, business, educational, labour, and professional leaders. The committees are the Canadian Economic Policy Committee, which has been concentrating on Canadian economic issues, especially in the area of trade, since 1961; the Canadian-American Committee, which has dealt with relations between Canada and the United States since 1957 and is jointly sponsored by HRI and the National Planning Association in Washington; and the British-North American Committee, formed in 1969 and sponsored jointly by the National Planning Association, the British-North American Research Association in London, and HRI. Each of the three committees meets twice a year to consider important current issues and to sponsor and review studies that contribute to a better public understanding of such issues.

In addition to taking over the publications of the three PPAC committees, HRI releases the work of its staff, and occasionally of outside authors, in four other publications: *Observations,* six or seven of which are published each year; *Policy Review and Outlook,* published annually; *Special Studies,* to provide detailed analysis of major policy issues; and *Commentaries*, to give wide circulation to the views of experts on issues of current Canadian interest.

HRI publications, including those of the Canadian-American Committee, are available from the Institute's offices, 2064 Sun Life Building, Montreal, Quebec H3B 2X7 (Tel. 514—879-1254).

The National Planning Association is a private, non-profit, non-political organization that carries on research and policy formulation in the public interest. NPA was founded during the great depression of the 1930s, when conflicts among the major economic groups — business, farmers, labor — threatened to paralyze national decision-making on the critical issues confronting American society. It was dedicated, in the words of its statement of purpose, to "getting [these] diverse groups to work together . . . to narrow areas of controversy and broaden areas of agreement. . . [and] to provide on specific problems concrete programs for action planned in the best traditions of a functioning democracy." NPA is committed to the view that the survival of a functioning American democracy under the increasingly rigorous conditions of the 20th century requires not only more effective government policies but also preservation of private economic initiative and the continuous development by the major private groups themselves of a consensus on how to cope with the problems confronting the nation at home and abroad.

NPA works through policy committees of influential and knowledgeable leaders from business, labor, agriculture, and the professions that make recommendations for dealing with domestic and international developments affecting the well-being of the United States. The research and writing for these committees are provided by NPA's professional staff and, as required, by outside experts. In addition, NPA's professional staff undertakes technical research, including preparation of economic and demographic projections for the national economy, states, and metropolitan areas; program planning and evaluation for government agencies; research on national goals and priorities; studies of manpower training, medical care, environmental protection, energy needs, and other economic and social problems confronting American society; and analyses of changing international realities and their implications for U.S. policies.

NPA publications, including those of the Canadian-American Committee, can be obtained from the Association's offices, 1606 New Hampshire Avenue, N.W., Washington, D.C. 20009 (Tel. 202—265-7685).

AC 41 / $3.00
PA 146
SBN 0-88806-017-3